The End of the Days

A Study in the Book of Daniel

By
Dr. Guy Lee, D.D.

The End of the Days
A Study in the Book of Daniel

By
Dr. Guy Lee, D.D.
37 Bill Presley Road
Cleveland, GA 30528
Phone: 706-865-4555

E-mail: **tometterlee@gmail.com**

© Guy Lee 2020

All rights reserved.

Printed in the United States of America
All Scripture quotations and references are from
the King James Version of the Holy Bible.

ISBN: 978-1-7344467-9-1

Published by:
The Old Paths Publications
142 Gold Flume Way
Cleveland, GA 30528
www.theoldpathspublications.com
TOP@theoldpathspublications.com

ACKNOWLEDGEMENTS

I want to thank Mrs. Sandie Pinkston for her time and excellent editorial assistance in the preparation of this manuscript, to Mrs. Brenda Nicholson for her assistance with the cover, and to my daughter, Linda Etterlee, for her time as well in working with Mrs. Pinkston and Mrs. Nicholson to make this book a reality.

This book is gratefully dedicated to Marvin and Barbara Anderson for all their support over the years of my ministry.

FOREWORD

Just as Daniel was a young Godly man who God used as a great leader of his time, so is our Daddy, Guy Lee. In looking back on our lives growing up in a Christian home, we can see just how much Daddy's life parallels with the life of Daniel.

As a young man, Daniel faced many difficult challenges, but he was faithful to pray and follow the leadership of the Lord no matter the cost. And so has it been in our Daddy's life as well. He taught not only by words, but by example. He always consulted the Word of God about all questions of life, and taught others to do the same.

And, just as Daniel was open and receptive to the message from the Lord about the end of time, so has Daddy been able to expound and relay that message in this current day. God has gifted Daddy with the ability to comprehend and explain the figurative and literal messages in the study of end time prophecy in the book of Daniel and also in Revelation.

If you struggle with understanding what is certain to come in the future, this book will be a tremendous help in making the troublesome times of today easier to understand and give you assurance that if you are saved, everything is going to be alright.

Daddy, thank you for teaching us about the Lord and how to study His Word. You and Mama are the best!

Linda and Beverly

TABLE OF CONTENTS

ACKNOWLEDGEMENTS 3
FOREWORD 4
TABLE OF CONTENTS 5
INTRODUCTION 16
Chapter 1 18
  1. The Captivity 18
    v.1 18
    v.2   Jehoiakim, King of Judah – he was 18
  2. The Choice 20
    vs.3-4 - Seven Requirements of those who were to be Chosen. They were to be: 21
    v.5 21
    v.6 21
  3. The Change 22
    v.7 22
  4. The Courage and Conviction 25
    v.8 25
    v.9 25
    v.10 26
    v.11 26
    v.12 26
    v.13 26
    v.14 26
  5. The Compensation 27
    v.15   The Radiant Faces 27
    v.16   The Removal of the Meat and Wine 27
    v.17 The Reward 27
  6. Commendation 28
    v.18 The Command '*bring them in.*' 28
    v.19 The Communication 28
    Examples in their exile 28
    v.20 The Completion of their three year Educational course 28
  7. Continuance 29
    v.21 29
Chapter 2 30
  1. The Dream 30
    v.1 30
    v.2 30
    v.3 32
    v.4 33

2. The Demand	33
v.5	33
v.6	34
v.7	34
3. The Delay	35
v.8	35
v.9	35
4. The Desperation	35
v.10	35
v.11	35
5. The Decree	36
v.12	36
v.13	36
6. The Decision	36
vs.14-16	36
vs.17	36
v.18	37
v.19	37
vs.20-23 Daniel Praised God	37
7. The Declaration	38
v.24 Daniel thinks about others	38
v.25 Arioch thinks about himself	38
v.26 The Failure of the Scholars	38
v.27	38
v.28 There is a God in Heaven	38
v.29	39
v.30	39
8. The Description	40
vs.31-33 The Terrible image	40
vs.34-35 The Stone	40
9. The Details	41
v.36	41
The First World Empire: Babylon The Head of Gold	41
v.37	41
v.38	41
The Golden City	41
The Period of the Babylonian Empire 605 – 539 B.C.	42
v.39	42
The Second World Empire: Medo-Persia	42
The Third World Empire: Greece : 331-146 B.C.	43
The Fourth World: Rome	43
v.40	43
The Final Form of Gentile World Dominion vs.41-43	44

TABLE OF CONTENTS

    When was the feet and toe stage to exist?............................ 45
    The Final World Empire: the Kingdom of Heaven.................. 45
    v.44.. 45
    v.45   The Stone.. 46
    10. The Declaration of Nebuchadnezzar............................... 46
    vs.46-49... 46
    v.47.. 46
    v.48-49... 46
Chapter 3... 48
The Image and the Furnace.. 48
    1. The Pride and Willfulness of the King................................... 48
    v.1   The Glory of Man.. 48
    v.2   The Government Officials 49
    2. The Proclamation to Worship by the King 49
    v.3   A Powerful Order Obeyed... 49
    vs.4-5   A Paid Orator... 49
    v.6.. 50
    v.7   A Pathetic (sad moving) Ordeal 50
    3.   The Personal Witness of the Three Hebrews................. 51
    The Dismay of the Majority... 51
    vs.8-12   The Watchers 51
    v.13-15... 51
    vs.16-18   The Witness... 52
    The Sovereignty of God.. 52
    4.   The Preservation and Welfare of the Three Hebrews....... 53
    Freedom in the Fire.. 53
    The Madness of the Monarch... 53
    v.19.. 53
    v.20.. 53
    v.21.. 53
    The Magnitude of the Miraculous... 54
    v.22.. 54
    v.23.. 54
    v.24.. 55
    The Mystery Man 55
    v.25.. 55
    v.26.. 55
    v.27.. 55
    The Musing of the Monarch... 56
    v.28.. 56
    v.29.. 56
    v.30.. 56
Chapter 4... 57

1. The Regenerate King Speaks...57
   1. Nebuchadnezzar Testimony...57
   v.1 57
   His Desire..57
   v.2   His Declaration 57
   v.3   His Devotion 58
   2. The Relating of the Dream 58
   v.4   The Prosperous King 58
   v.5   The Dream of the King..58
   vs.6-7   The Professional Group...................................59
   vs.8-9   The Proposition is Put to Daniel.......................59
   vs.10-12   The Provision 60
   v.13   The Participant...61
   v.14   The Power 61
   v.15   The Prospect 62
   v.16   The Period of Time...62
   v.17   The Preeminence of God 62
   v.18   The Powerless *Wise Men*..64
   3. The Revelation of the Dream..64
   v.19   The Astonishment of Daniel 64
   The Assessment of Daniel 64
   vs.20-21 64
   vs.22-23 64
   vs.24-25 65
   v.26 65
   v.27   The Appeal of Daniel..65
   4. The Rebellion of Nebuchadnezzar...................................66
   The Accomplishments of Nebuchadnezzar 66
   vs.28-29   Procrastination 66
   v.30   Pride...66
   v.31.a The Proclamation...67
   5. The Retribution of God..67
   v.31.b The Announcement from Heaven 67
   vs.32-33   The Animal-like Characteristic 67
   6. The Restoration 68
   v.34   The Salvation of God..68
   v.35   The Sovereignty of God 68
   v.36   The Seeking Counselors and Lords........................69
   v.37   The Satisfaction of Nebuchadnezzar 69
Chapter 5..**72**
   1. Belshazzar's Feast..72
   Deception – Drunkenness..72
   v.1 72

TABLE OF CONTENTS

    vs.2-3   The Defilers 73
    v.4   The Depraved 73
  2. Belshazzar's Fear 74
    The Fingers 74
    v.5 74
    The Fear 74
    v.6 74
    v.7 75
    The Failure 75
    v.8 75
    v.9   the Perplexed wise Men 75
    The Faithful 76
    v.10 76
    v.11 76
    v.12   Recommendation 76
    The Queen's evaluation of Daniel 77
  3. Belshazzar's Failure 77
    v.13   The Requirement 77
    v.14   The Recollection 78
    v.15   The Readily Confession 78
    v.16   The Reward 78
    v.17   The Refusal 79
    v.18   The Review 79
    v.19 79
    v.20 79
    v.21 79
    v.22   The Rebuke 79
    v.23 80
    v.24   The Revelation 80
    v.25 80
    v.26 80
    v.27 80
    v.28 81
    v.29   The Robing 81
  4. Belshazzar's Fall 81
    v.30 81
    v.31 81
Chapter 6 82
  1. Daniel's Conduct 82
    v.1 82
    v.2 82
  2. Daniel's Character 83
    v.3   the *Excellent Spirit* in Daniel 84

Daniel was Faultless (not corrupt) 84
　　　v.4　　Daniel was Faithful 84
　　　v.5　　Daniel's God 84
　3. Daniel's Conspirators 85
　　　v.6　　The Plot 85
　　　vs.7-8　　The Plan 85
　　　v.9 85
　4. Daniel's Courage 86
　　　v.10　　Daniel an example of prayer. 86
　5. Daniel's Crisis 87
　　　v.11　　The Assemble Enemies 87
　　　v.12　　The Answer of the King 87
　　　v.13　　The Accusers 87
　　　v.14　　The Angry King 88
　　　v.15 88
　　　The Able Deliverer 88
　　　v.16　　The Silences of Daniel 88
　　　v.17　　The Seal; The Signet. 89
　6. Daniel's Compensation 89
　　　v.18　　The Miserable Night 89
　　　The Morning Discovery 89
　　　v.19 89
　　　v.20 90
　　　v.21 90
　　　v.22 90
　　　v.23　　The Mighty God of Daniel 90
　　　v.24　　The Merciless Execution 90
　　　The Magnificent Dominion 91
　　　1. Man's Dominion 91
　　　The Earth 91
　　　v.25　　The Kings Decree to all the earth. 92
　　　v. 26　　The Decree 92
　　　2. God's Dominion 92
　　　v.27 92
　　　v.28　　The Prosperity of Daniel 93
Chapter 7 94
The Four Great Beasts 94
　1. The Introduction of the vision 94
　　　v.1　　When Daniel Dreamed 94
　　　What Daniel Dreamed. 94
　　　v.2　　Striving Winds 94
　　　v.3　　The Stormy Waves 95
　2. The Information in the Vision 95

TABLE OF CONTENTS

1. The First Beast: a Lion; The Babylonian Empire (Reign 66 to 70 yrs.) 95
   v.4   The Ravenous Lion 95
2. The Second Beast: a Bear; The Medo-Persia Empire (Reign 207 yrs.) 96
   v.5   The Rapacious (to take by force) Bear 96
3. The Third Beast – The Grecian Empire   (Reign just over 300 years) 96
   v.6   The Rapid Leopard 97
4. The Fourth Beast – The Roman Empire 97
   v.7   The Raging Beast 97
5. The Restoration of the Roman Empire 99
   v.7   The Ten Horns 99
   v.8   The Tiny Horn 99
6. The Return of Jesus Christ 99
   v.9   The Ancient of Days 99
   v.10 100
   v.11   The Awful Retribution on the Little Horn 100
   v.12   As for the Rest of Beasts 100
7. The Reign of the Redeemer 101
   v. 13 101
   v.14 101
3. The Interpretation of the Vision 101
   1. Daniels Puzzled Request 101
      v.15   His Grief 101
      v.16   His Guidance 101
   2. Daniel's Prophetic Review 102
      1. The Five Kingdoms 102
      2. The Fourth Kingdom 102
      v.19 102
      v.20 103
      v.21 103
      v.22 103
      vs.23-24 104
      v.26 105
   3. The Fifth Kingdom 106
      v.27 106
   3. Daniel's Personal Reaction 106
      v.28 106
Chapter 8 108
The Persian Ram and the Greek Goat 108
1. Mark the time and Place 108
   v.1   The Time 108

v.2 The Place 108
2. The Three Personages of the 108
Vision and the Little Horn 108
   The First Personage 108
   The Ram symbol of Persia 108
   v. 3 108
   v.4 The Powerful Hold 109
   The Second Personage 110
   v.5 110
   v. 6 110
   v.7 110
   v.8 110
   The Third Personage 111
   v.9 The little horn expands his borders........................... 111
   The time period permitted 112
   v.13 112
   v.14 112
3. The Troubled Prophet 113
   The vision interpreted 113
   vs.15-16 113
   v.17 113
   v.18 113
4. The Terrible Power of the Persecutor 113
   v.19 113
   v.20 114
   v.21 114
   v.22 114
   The King of Fierce Countenance... 114
   v.23 The Emergence of a Person.................................... 114
   v.24 The Enduement with a Power.................................. 115
   v.25 The Enactment of his Policy 115
   The Effects of the Vision 116
   v.26 116
Chapter 9 117
1. The Prediction of Jeremiah... 117
   The Promptings of Prayer 117
   v.1 117
2. The Prayer of Daniel 117
   v.3 What did Daniel Do 117
   The Particulars in the Prayer.. 118
   v.4 118
   vs.7-10 118
   v.11 119

TABLE OF CONTENTS

v.12 119
v.13 119
v.14 119
vs.15-19   The Petition in Prayer 120
vs.20-23   The Power in the Prayer 120
3. The Prophecy of the   Seventy Weeks 121
    v.24   A Definition of the 70 years. 121
    The Division of the 70 Weeks 123
    v.25   We have seventy (70) weeks in verse 24. Gabriel explains that the seventy (70) weeks are divided into three (3) sections in verses 24 and 25. 123
    v.26   What will happen after the 69 weeks? 124
    v.27   A Description of the 70th week 126
Chapter 10 128
    1. Daniel's condition 128
    The Revelation 128
    v.1 128
    The Resolution 128
    v.2 128
    v.3 128
    2. A Crucial Question 129
    Who was this Heavenly being? 129
    v.4 129
    1. The Terror 129
    vs.5-6 129
    v.7 129
    v.8 129
    2. The Trance 129
    v.9 129
    3. The Communication of the Certain Man 130
    v.10   The Touch 130
    v.11   The Trembling 130
    v.12   Total Surrender 131
    4. The Conflict 131
    v.13   The Rejection 131
    The Response 132
    v.14   The Revelation 133
    v.15   The Reaction 133
    v.16 133
    v.17 133
    v.18 133
    v.19 133
    The Resolution 133

- v.20 134
- v.21 134
- **Chapter 11** **136**
  - 1. The Continuation 136
    - v.1 136
    - v.2 136
  - 2. The Conquer 137
    - v.3 137
    - v.4 137
  - 3. The Conflict 138
    - v.5   The king of the south 138
    - v.6   A Political Marriage 138
    - Wars of Revenge 139
    - v.7 139
    - v.8 139
    - v.9 139
    - A Tireless War 139
    - v.10 139
    - v.11 140
    - v.12 140
    - v.13 140
    - v.14 140
    - v.15 140
    - v.16 141
    - v.17 141
    - v.18 141
    - v.19 141
    - v.20 141
  - 4. The Cruel Antiochus Epiphanes 142
    - v.21 142
    - v.22 142
    - v.23 142
    - v.24 142
    - v.25 143
    - v.26 143
    - v.27 143
    - v.28 143
    - v.29 143
    - v.30 143
    - v.31 144
    - v.32 144
    - v.33 144
    - v.34-35 144

TABLE OF CONTENTS

   5. The Coming of the Antichrist..145
      1. The Character of the Antichrist 145
      v.36... 145
      v.37... 146
      vs.38-39.. 146
      2. The Conflicts of the Antichrist 146
      v.40... 146
      v.41   The Center Stage 147
      v.42   the Doom of Egypt... 148
      v.43   The Power and Riches.. 148
      v.44   the Gathering Storm.. 148
      v.45   the Doom of the Antichrist... 149
Chapter 12..150
   1. The Great Tribulation... 150
   v.1.. 150
   2. The Triumph of the Saints.. 150
      v.2   First Resurrection 151
      Second Resurrection.. 151
      v.3   The Wise... 151
   3. The Time... 152
      v.4   The Sealed Book.. 152
      The Scene at the River.. 153
      v.5.. 153
      v.6.. 153
      v.7   The Solemn Oath 154
   4. The Terminating 155
      v.8   The Puzzled Prophet.. 155
      v.9   The Proper Time 156
      v.10   The Purified.. 156
      Three Periods of time.. 156
      v.11.. 156
      v.12.. 157
      v.13   The Personal Prophecy 157
Bibliography   159

INTRODUCTION

To use this book as a study help of the Book of Daniel, it is recommended you use it alongside of an open Bible as all the Scripture references throughout the book are not written out verbatim et literatim.

I am grateful to the Lord for His help in the completion of this book on the book of Daniel. It is my earnest hope that it will be a help to the Lord's people in a further appreciation for the Word of God.

> II Timothy 2:2 *"And the things that thou hast heard of me among many witnesses, the same commit thou to faithful men, who shall be able to teach others also."*

In this verse, we have a multiplication principle. Here is the ultimate goal of the ministry – pass it on.

As a student, Timothy was taught the Word of God by Paul. As a Pastor, Timothy must now teach those things to other faithful men. This was the principle and practice predicated in

> Psalms 145:4 *"One generation shall praise thy works to another, and shall declare thy mighty acts."*

I am just one link in the chain passing on what God has taught in His Word, and passing on what I was taught by faithful preachers and teachers of the Word of God.

The more deeply I have delved into the study of the books of Daniel and Revelation, the more firmly convinced I have become that these books need to be preached more

INTRODUCTION

than ever before, and should be engaging the attention of the Church in a larger measure.

Our Lord's last message to His Church, a message given after His ascension to heaven, is found in Revelation, which is a continuation of the book of Daniel. Yet, few sermons are preached in our pulpits that are based on this message, the importance of which can hardly be overestimated.

No claim is made for scholarship or originality. Please receive it in the spirit in which it is written; a desire to help.

Chapter 1

1. The Captivity

v.1   Critics say there is a conflict between Daniel 1:1 and Jeremiah 25:1. Jeremiah points out the Babylonian captivity occurred *in the fourth year of Jehoiakim*'s reign. Daniel declares it happened *in the third year*. Critics do not have a leg to stand on when they say this is a contradiction. Both statements are correct.

The conquest began near the close of the third year and was finished in the fourth year of the reign of Jehoiakim. Also in 2 Kings 23:36 we are told that Jehoiakim **reigned eleven years**. So he is a careless reader who calls it a contradiction, for it was in this 'third year' that Jehoiakim's reign came to an end. A glance at 2 Kings 24:1 will lead us to see that it was in 'the third year' of Jehoiakim's reign as a subject king of Nebuchadnezzar, and not in the third year of his reign as reckoned from the beginning.

v.2   Jehoiakim, King of Judah – he was
- An **Evil** king. *2 Kings 23:37*
- He committed an unpardonable sin. *2 Kings 24:4*
- He is known as "The king who burnt the Bible", *Jer.36:32* after cutting the prophetic Word into pieces with a **penknife**. *Jer.36:23*
- Note: This is what many are doing today. They are reading the Bible and cutting out what they do not like. Also this is the reason today why there is such uproar over the Ten Commandments. The commands condemned man's wicked ways and they do not like it.

CHAPTER 1

And **with part of the vessels of the house of God** King Nebuchadnezzar:
- used them in the worship of the Babylonian god Marduk.
- tried to show that his gods were more powerful than the captive's God. (The vessels were later returned to Jerusalem by Cyrus *Ezra 1:7-11* and the rest by Darius. *Ezra 6:5*)

[have been asked if I still preach from the King James Bible - and I say "Yes, The old scout follows the old trail".]

NOTATIONS:
Three Invasions resulting in Captivity
A study of the Books of Kings and Chronicles will show that there were at least three invasions of Jerusalem and Judah by Nebuchadnezzar, king of Babylon.

First Invasion (606-604 B.C.)
2 Kings 24:1-5; 2 Chr.36:5-8; Jer.36
Daniel and his three friends Hananiah, Mishael, and Azariah were carried off to Babylon.

Second Invasion (598-597 B.C.)
2 Kings 24:6-17; Ezek.1:1-2
Ezekiel was carried to Babylon.

Third Invasion (587 B.C.)
2 Kings 24:17-20; 25:1-21; Jer.34:1-22; 39:1-18
This was under the reign of Zedekiah.

A careful reading of these scriptures listed above will provide us with the details.

The Reasons for the Captivity
1. Disobeying God's Word
God had commanded them to let the land lie fallow every **seventh year**. *Lev.25:3-6*
For seventy Sabbaths they disobeyed God. *2.Chr.36:21*
(This takes us back to the time of Israel's first king, Saul. *1 Sam.9* 70 x 7 = 490; For 490 years they had disobeyed God's Word, now judgment has come, and they must pay the price.) So God let them be carried away captive to Babylon for seventy years. God is not playing games with us in the Bible – so do not take Him lightly.

2. Idolatry
They found a strange fascination with idols of the pagan nations around them. *1 Kings 11:5; 12:28; 16:31; 18:19; 2 Kings 21:3-5; 2 Chr.28:1-4.* They had been solemnly warned of God's coming judgment upon them because of their idolatry. *Jer.7:24; 8:3; 44:20-23* When the Word of God is ignored and violated - Divine judgment sooner or later is inevitable.

2. The Choice

Daniel and his Companions Chosen
Nebuchadnezzar recognized the value of training young people.
Parents and Church - do you see the value and need of winning our young people to Christ and to train them in the way and the work of God?!

CHAPTER 1

vs.3-4 - Seven Requirements of those who were to be Chosen. They were to be:

1. **of royal or noble parentage** v.3
2. **without blemish** v.4 By which I understand physical blemish; They were not to be in any sense physically deformed.
3. **well favoured** - The reference is to their personal appearance. Their personal appearance was to be attractive.
4. **skilful in all wisdom** - or intelligent in all branches of knowledge.
5. **cunning in knowledge** - or equipped with knowledge.
6. **understanding science** - expert in learning; able to impart instruction.
7. **and such as had ability in them to stand in the king's palace** - or competent to take their place in the kings palace.

And whom they might teach the learning and the tongue of the Chaldeans.

The literature of Babylon involved learning magic, arts, incantations, divination, mythology, and the religion of Babylon; All would help to wean them from God's literature 'the Old Testament Scriptures' as written.

v.5 The Monarch saw in them great promise but he knew they had to be weaned from their former faith and belief if they were to be useful in Babylon.

v.6 Four young men from *Judah*; *Daniel, Hananiah, Mishael, and Azariah*. They were probably 16-17 years of age. These four young men were singled out, although surely there were others in the program.

Why are the others not mentioned? Did they cave in to the pressure because they were not willing to pay the price, and so their names are not mentioned in God's Word?

Each of their names were an eloquent testimony to the power and grace of God.

> **Daniel** – means "God is my Judge"
> **Hananiah** – means "the Lord is Gracious"
> **Mishael** – means "Who is what God is" or
>   "Who is comparable to God?"
> **Azariah** – means "The Lord is my Help"

Each name had either 'God' or "The Lord" in it.

We are to bear a precious name – 'Christian'. Do we honor Him, whose name it proclaims - before a godless world - by guarding our testimony, our daily walk? Daniel and his friends can teach us many lessons here.

3. The Change

v.7 Their names were changed from Hebrew to Babylonian names.
1. **Daniel was changed to *Belteshazzar*,** meaning "Prince or Keeper of Bel's Treasures". Bel was the chief god of the Babylonians. Daniel being the noted of the four youth's was probably given this name because of this quality. Daniel's personal name is mentioned some 75 times in Daniel while his Babylonian name, ***Belteshazzar*** is mentioned 10 times.
2. **Hananiah was changed to *Shadrach*;** meaning "inspired or illuminated by the Sun god (sun god in Babylon).

CHAPTER 1

3. **Mishael was changed to *Meshach***; meaning "Skek" A pagan name meaning 'who is like Venus'.
4. **Azariah was changed to *Abed-nego***; meaning 'Slave or servant of Nego". Nego meant 'shinning fire' and was the second dominant god of the Babylonians; the Babylonian god of wisdom, connected with the planet Mercury.

A tyrant may change ones' name but not the nature of one true to God.

It was the full intention of Nebuchadnezzar to destroy every trace of connection between these young men and their people, land, and religion.

There is a movement in America to remove God from every phase of society. They say 'the Bible is not trustworthy' and 'there are many ways to God'. Not So! Jesus is the only way to God.

1. *I am the way*
2. *the truth*
3. *and the life*
4. *no man cometh unto the Father but by me*
   John 14:6
5. **The only saving name** Acts 4:12
6. **The only door** John 10:9
7. **The only mediator** 1 Tim.2:5

Instead they promote that which is against nature: same sex marriage; homosexuality. This is an ***abomination*** to God. Lev.18:22-24; Rom.1:24-32

Two points of likeness that will repeat themselves' in the last days:

1. Days of Noe
1. **wicked** Gen.6:5
2. **evil** Gen.6:5
3. **corrupt** Gen.6:11
4. **filled with violence** Gen.6:11

The affairs also list the routine of everyday life.
Men were: Matt.24:37-39:
1. *eating*
2. *drinking*
3. *marrying*
4. indifferent – no time for God
5. ignorant <u>and they **knew not** until the flood came and took them all away</u>. This indicates that the last generation will be totally unprepared for the second coming of Jesus Christ.

2. Days of Lot Gen.19:1-38
The iniquity of Sodom Ezek.16:49-50
1. *pride*
2. *fullness of bread*
3. *abundance of idleness*
4. neglected the *poor and needy*
5. *haughty*
6. *committed abomination*
   i.e. homosexuality: ***therefore I (God) took them away as I saw good.*** This is Judgment.

The affairs also list the routine of everyday life in Lot's day Luke 17:28-30
Men:
1. *eat*
2. *drank*
3. *bought*
4. *sold*

5. *planted*
6. *builded*

7. Judgment on Sodom - *the same day that Lot went out of Sodom it (God) rained fire and brimstone from heaven, and destroyed them all.*
8. *Even thus shall it be in the day when the Son of man is revealed.*

In the days of both Noah and Lot - the people ignored God and carried on with their lives as they always did. So too, people now go about business as usual, even though storm clouds are gathering again.

4. The Courage and Conviction

v.8 Since Daniel's heart was in tune with God – the Lord would not forsake him at this critical hour. Daniel's objection to eat the king's meats was not just a teenage whim; it was based on sound convictions.

Daniel held firm to the original scriptural principles of Leviticus 11 where certain things eaten by the Gentiles were called '*unclean*'.

The food set before him was from animals that were slaughtered ceremonially and offered to the Babylonian gods. No wonder *Daniel purposed in his heart that he would not defile himself with the portion of the king's meat* and drink. So Daniel and his three friends were doubly exercised – by the Word of God and by conscience.

v.9 Daniel showed the love of God to Ashpenaz - and the Lord gave the Babylonian official real love for the young captive from Judah.

v.10 Ashpenaz feared for his life if he granted Daniel's request: *then shall ye make me endanger my head to the king.* He was personally responsible to the king for these young men; and should any ill effects result from altering their diet, Nebuchadnezzar could have him beheaded. He wanted to grant Daniel's request but could not. He feared that if the four Jewish youths abstained from the king's diet, they would appear unhealthier than the other students when it was time to be examined by the king. While he did not openly want to grant Daniel's request and thereby rescind Nebuchadnezzar's command, he could quietly condone that Daniel and Melzar decide this matter. (Melzar was Ashpenaz's appointed assistant *v.11.*)

v.11 Daniel approached Melzar with a proposition....

v.12 .....that he would allow them a trial period of *ten days*, during which they would be fed only *pulse*: food made of ground seeds, fruits, and vegetables mixed with water.

v.13 After ten days a comparison could be made between them and the young men who ate from the king's table. Depending on how the comparison came out, it could then be decided on what course of action to take. Daniel was so certain of his case and his victory that he dared to say the courageous words *and as thou seeth, deal with thy servants*. We are seeing here Daniel's true miraculous faith in action. He simply believed a miracle would happen to him and his three friends. His faith rested only in God, and he was not put to shame.

v.14 *So he* (Melzar) *consented to them in this matter, and proved them ten days.*

CHAPTER 1

There is one special trait in Daniel which we observe again and again. It is that he knew how to captivate men's minds in a special way. This is a unique gift which becomes ours only by God's sovereign will and grace. Daniel possessed this gift to a high degree, for whether he stood before his friends, before high officials, over against his conquerors, or other mighty rulers, he always commanded respect and people bowed to him. This gift would serve him well in the future.

5. The Compensation

v.15　The Radiant Faces
God's grace shone even more brightly in this feeding miracle. He most clearly showed here that His favor strengthens more that the choicest food.

v.16　The Removal of the Meat and Wine
Melzar was sufficiently impressed with Daniel and his three friends that he followed through with Daniel's proposal. So **Melzar took away the portion of their meat and wine** and let them continue with their vegetable diet.

v.17　The Reward
God took care of Daniel, Hananiah, Mishael, and Azariah because of their commitment to His Word and His Spirit.
God gave these four young men:
- **knowledge** Prov.1:1-7
- **skill in all learning**; an ability to grasp things readily.
- **Wisdom** Prov.24:3-4; Jas.1:5-17; Ezek.38:3; Col.2:3

- **and Daniel had understanding in all visions and dreams.**

6. Commendation

v.18 The Command 'bring them in.'
This is Graduation Day! At the end of the course (three years) this was the final examination before the king. These four young men had to give an account to Nebuchadnezzar, just as we too must **give account of himself to God.** Rom.14:12

'Exiles from the promise land but not from the promises of God'.

v.19 The Communication
'and the king communed with them'. The wisdom, knowledge, understanding and skill they received from the true God would be needed in the days that lay ahead. All that they experienced was preparation for ministry: the fiery furnace, the den of lions, and tests of a heathen court, the jealousies of magicians and astrologers, the wise men of Babylon, and the glory of the Babylonian empire.

Examples in their exile

v.20 The Completion of their three year Educational course
God helped Daniel and his friends to learn their subjects well. This included the gift of discerning what was true and false knowledge. To Daniel was added the

CHAPTER 1

discerning of dreams and visions; to be *ten times better than all of the magicians and astrologers.* These young men had to buckle down and study.

Excelled all standards in exile

If preachers want to be blessed of God they must learn their Bibles well and live a life of prayer. There is no easy road to success. There is a price to pay. The Bible tells us to *Study to shew thyself approved unto God, a workman that needeth not to be ashamed, rightly dividing the word of truth.* 2.Tim. 2:15

7. Continuance

<u>v.21</u> *Daniel continued* (in his role) *even unto the first year of King Cyrus* of Persia (536 B.C.). That is Daniel continued right through the 70 years of the Babylonian captivity to the decree of Cyrus to release the Jewish captives, rebuild the Temple of the Lord, and release the city of Jerusalem to be rebuilt. All this would be, as will be seen, in fulfillment of the prophecies given some 100 years before hand. *Isa.44:28-45:6; 2 Chron.36:22-23; Ezra 1:1*

Jeremiah had foretold the period of the captivity to be for 70 years. *Jer.25:8-14; 29:10-14*

God blessed Daniel with a long life; He lived beyond the first year of Cyrus *Dan.9:1-2; 10:1.* and would have been approximately 90 years of age. Read the following Scriptures: Exodus 20:12; Eph.6:1-3.

Daniel and his three friends are a picture of the faithful remnant in the tribulation days. *Rev.7:4-8; 14:1*

Chapter 2

This dream of Nebuchadnezzar, occurring early in his reign, was one of the most important dreams of all time, since it predicted the history of the Gentile world through four successive empires. It also included the prophecy of Christ's Millennial kingdom.

1. The Dream

v.1 The dream made a lasting impression upon the mind of Nebuchadnezzar. Conscience, which makes cowards of all wrong doers, was troubling the wicked king. His mind was distressed; *his spirit was troubled.*

Note: Mark the expression "*Wherewith his spirit was troubled*" – with the words 'violently agitated'.

His sleep brake from him. He was not only agitated but found himself on through the hours of darkness that his sleep had gone from him. There is no terror like the soul gripped in fear – no terror like the terror of many sleepless hours - far more troubling at night than in the daytime, for darkness adds to his terror. Here, in his trouble and agitation he could find no end. Nebuchadnezzar – the 'troubler' of God's people – but God was the 'troubler' of Nebuchadnezzar.

v.2 Nebuchadnezzar calls all the wise men of Babylon to his court. Some of the various groups of wise men are listed here.
   1. **Magicians** - they practiced magic; followed superstitious rites and ceremonies; acting as fortune-tellers. *Ex. 7:11; Deut. 18:9-14; Lev. 19:26-31; Isa. 47:12-13*

CHAPTER 2

2. **Astrologers** – Pretended to foretell future events by the study of the stars. Superstition even as the monthly prognosticators of our times forbidden by Scripture. *Isa.47:13* The Bible permits Astronomy (study of the stars), but not Astrology (worship of the stars).
3. **Sorcerers** – Pretended to hold communication with the dead, even as spiritualist in our times. Sorcerers are also involved in making and use of drug – enchantments. *Isa.8:19-20; Acts 13:6-8; Rev.9:21; 18:23* Our word 'Pharmacy' comes from the Greek word 'Pharmakia' - maker, user and enchanter with drugs.
4. **Chaldeans** - A sect of Philosophers, who made science and divinations their study. They claimed to be able to obtain supernatural knowledge. These were the wise men of Babylon. These men were the wisest of the wise at that time. Their calculation of the length of a year differed from modern science by only 23 minutes and 55 seconds.

NOTATION: **Modern Babylon times**
In today's society, we are living in a modern day 'Babylon' situation, even as Daniel and his three friends. Society throughout the world reveals the desperate cry for 'guidance' in some supernatural way.

This is seen in the multitudinous ways that society seeks guidance from the world of the occult. The world of the occult is Satan's way and method of false guidance.

The whole purpose is to side-track mankind from the true guidance from God, through Christ, by the power of the Holy Spirit.

What the Church needs today is the wisdom of God. Paul tells us the **world by wisdom** (worldly wisdom) **knew not God** *1 Cor.1:21* - we are not saved by worldly wisdom but by Jesus Christ. **But of him are ye in Christ Jesus who of God is made unto wisdom, and righteousness, and sanctification, and redemption.** *1 Cor.1:30*

Three Classes *1Cor.1:26*
The call is not based on man's position
1. **The Wise** – Refers to the intellect of men – what they have learned.
2. **The Mighty** - Points to the influence of men – that which they have gain through political or military conquest.
3. **The Noble** – Denotes the inheritance of men – the status of birth into well-known families.

Note: Paul did not say 'Not <u>any</u> of the wise, mighty, and noble are called, but **not <u>many</u>** of them.' I quote H.A. Ironside "Saul (Paul) of Tarsus stands out himself in vivid contrast, and one who, whether saved are not, would have had some great place among the people of that day, but he is the one who writes the words that we have been considering, and he counted himself among the base things, things which are despised, things which are not."

<u>v.3</u>   At sundry times and divers manners God revealed His right will to men. The king had dreamed, was disturbed as a result, and wanted to know what the dream meant.

- **Pharaoh's dream** of the fat and lean kine (cattle) was skillfully interpreted by Joseph *Gen.41*

CHAPTER 2

- **Jacobs dream** of a ladder - a foreshadowing of Jesus - who was to bridge the gulf between a Holy God and sinful man.

v.4 The highest of these four orders, the Chaldeans, or the wise men replied, "tell us the dream". Their living depended on the approval of the king. They were fed out of the treasury. They were particularly anxious to please him.

- The Chaldeans spoke to the king in Syriack (Aramaic), the ancient language of Syria, and substantially identical with Chaldaic; the language of Babylonia.
- The Aramaic language was at that time the most common tongue used for trading purposes throughout the world. From Dan.2:24 – 7:28 Daniel wrote in this language rather than Hebrew. This section basically concerns the Gentiles.
- The Hebrew sections are written to the Jews, to the Hebrew people, in their language. Together, God uses both languages to let His truth be known.

The Chaldeans made their typical reply '*O king live forever*', seeking to appease the king and encourage him to reveal the contents of the dream.

2. The Demand

v.5 The wise men say to the king "tell us the dream and we'll tell you the interpretation". But Nebuchadnezzar refuses to do so. He tells them '*the thing is gone from me*'. He threatened '*If you will not make known the dream with the interpretation*, all of you will be killed'.

Here is a dictator who overreacts to his fears. He is saying, you tell me what I want to know, or you're all dead.

   Here we see the display of the king's
- Arrogance
- Violence
- Rage
- Recklessness

He threatened with
- Death
- Dismemberment
- Disgrace

v.6 Here he promises that if these 'counterfeit interpreters of dreams' would recall or relate to him the dream that he had, and interpret it to him, he would give them **gifts, and rewards, and great honour**. He then appealed to them to **show me the dream**, or describe it vividly, so he would recognize it; then give him the meaning of it, to relieve or drive away his fears.

   The king was
- Depressed
- Agitated
- Anxious

v.7 The wise men appealed a second time for the king to relate the dream. They had pledged to interpret it - for they intended to 'manufacture a meaning' for the dream - if they could get him to relate it to them.

CHAPTER 2

3. The Delay

v.8 The king knew that he had asked them to do a hard thing, but he could not change his mind.

v.9 So he started to get angry and said they were trying to avoid his threat to kill them. He said they were planning together to tell him lies - hoping that he would change his mind.

Astrologers believe that the stars and planets have an influence on men, so they claim that some days are better than others. This was one of their bad days according to what they taught.

In ancient near East, much was made of lucky and unlucky days. Sadly, our own culture seems to be increasingly caught up in such occult beliefs.

4. The Desperation

v.10 The wise men's final desperate appeal to reason may be paraphrased "you are being unfair to organized magicians!" *There is no king, lord, nor ruler that asked such things at any magician, or astrologer, or Chaldean.*

v.11 They conclude their argument by stating that no human being could meet the kings demands; that if the answer comes, it will be by supernatural means. This paves the way for Daniel.

5. The Decree

v.12 Nebuchadnezzar blew up! He is *angry and very furious, and commanded to destroy all the wise men of Babylon.* When people are angry, they are wrong; and when they are wrong, they are even angrier and more frustrated, and they make decisions that ultimately lead to destruction.

v.13 The orders go out – *and the decree went forth that the wise men should be slain.* This included Daniel and his three friends. Satan is making a bid for the destruction of Daniel and his holy companions. *Be sober be valiant because the adversary the Devil, as a roaring Lion, walketh about, seeking whom he may devour.* 1 Pet.5:8

6. The Decision

vs.14-16 With confidence in God and using the language of faith, Daniel wisely answered Arioch. Daniel no doubt recognized that this was an opportunity for God to demonstrate His sovereign will and purpose to all concerned. Daniel's wise counsel included a question about the hastiness of the king's decree and a request for time to obtain the contents and interpretation of the dream.

Daniel's request for time was not considered stalling, and Nebuchadnezzar granted him the request.

vs.17 Daniel goes to his friends Hananiah, Mishael, and Azariah (their Hebrew names). And told them what had happened and how their lives were at stake.

CHAPTER 2

v.18 Immediately they go to God in prayer. It is left to us to imagine what kind of prayer meeting this was. It certainly would not be a half-hearted, fatalistic kind of prayer meeting. It would be earnest, sincere, faith-filled and urgent.

Unity in this prayer was essential; Two or three agreeing would ensure an answer to the prayer. Matt.18:19. There was united church prayer; Acts 2:42 there were many gathered together in a home to pray for Peter; Acts 12:5-12; and Paul *kneeled down, and prayed with them all.* Acts 20:36

There is power in united prayer.

v.19 The secret of the dream was revealed to one man, Daniel - not to the other three. There should be no jealousy when God takes up one man, even though others may be just as well qualified and faithful.

If you can rejoice at the success of another - you have *pure religion*. James 1:27

vs.20-23   Daniel Praised God

- *Blessed be the name of God for ever and ever: for wisdom and might are his.*
- *He changeth the times and the seasons.*
- *He removeth kings, and setteth up kings.*
- *He giveth wisdom unto the wise, and knowledge to them that know understanding.*
- *He revealeth the deep and secret things.*
- *He knoweth what is in the darkness, and the light dwelleth with him.*
- And Daniel *thanked...God...who hast given me wisdom and might.*

7. The Declaration

v.24 Daniel thinks about others
His prime concern is for the safety and well-being of other people. He is a humanitarian in the best sense of the word. He selflessly thinks about his fellow-man.

v.25 Arioch thinks about himself
Officer Arioch wrongly claimed credit for having found an interpreter for the king's dream. Actually it was Daniel who "'went to Arioch". Arioch evidently expected to be highly rewarded for finding someone who could alleviate the kings' agitation.

v.26 The Failure of the Scholars
Nebuchadnezzar gives audience to Daniel. Daniel goes in and stands before the king because all the wise men and experienced counselors of state had been unable to answer the king. The king expressed surprise that a man as young as Daniel should be able to meet the challenge.
- *Art thou able to make known unto me the dream which I have seen, and the interpretation thereof?*

v.27 The solution to the problem, the power of prediction, lay with the God of Heaven and not with the useless gods of Babylon.

v.28 There is a God in Heaven
Daniel testified humbly that *there is a God in Heaven that revealeth secrets.* He is the one who had made known to Nebuchadnezzar – a Gentile unbeliever – what was going to take place *in the latter days.*

God has plans for the latter days of Israel Gen.41:1; Deut.31:29; Dan.2:28 which will climax with Christ's return to

CHAPTER 2

earth *Rev.19:11-21* and being received by His people; *Hosea 3:5; Micah 4:1; Joel 2:28-29* the time of Jacobs's trouble. *Jer.30:7* The Tribulation time runs from Revelation chapter 6 through chapter 19.

Jesus ushered in the 'Last Days" with His death, Resurrection, and Ascension to Heaven. *Heb.1:2; 1 Pet.1:20* So we are living now in the period of time when God is calling a people out of the world to make up His body; the Church. *2 Tim.1:9; 1 Pet.2:9* The last days of the Church include perilous times; *2 Tim.3.1* the apostasy, and the rise of scoffers and deniers of the Bible; *2 Pet.3:1* - and the period will end when Christ raptures His Church to Heaven. *1 Thes.4:13-18* The Church will be raptured to Heaven <u>before</u> the Tribulation. *1 Thes.1:10; 5:9* Do you think there is no answer to your problems? **There is a God in Heaven.**

<u>**v.29**</u> The **Secret** is spoken of as a **dream**, a **vision**, and the king's '**thoughts**' - all of which originated with the God of Heaven. God is showing Nebuchadnezzar what would come to pass both hereafter and in the latter days.

<u>**v.30**</u> Daniel -like Joseph before Pharaoh- *Gen.41* evidences great humility. He told him **the secret was not revealed to me for any wisdom I have,** any more than anyone else. It was revealed to him for Nebuchadnezzar's sake, that he might know that God is sovereign in the affairs of earthly kingdoms. It was also revealed for the preservation of Daniel and his three companions from the death penalty. The rest of the wise men of Babylon were saved by this divine act.

Daniel is an outstanding example of those who are greatly blessed of God. He will bless and use those who honor Him instead of reaping glory for themselves.

8. The Description

The figure of a man was employed here by God to make known what would transpire during mans' day; the age in which mortal man rules the earth. Here in one panoramic sweep, the whole history of civilization is spread before us, from the days of Nebuchadnezzar, to the end of time.

vs.31-33   The Terrible image
In these verses Daniel tells the dream he had received to the king: The king saw a **great image**, **bright** and **excellent**, **terrible in form**, standing before him. It was frightening in its appearance, glistening in beauty, fearsome and alarming.
 1. It's **head was of fine gold**
 2. It's **breast and arms** were of **silver**
 3. It's **belly and thighs** were **brass** (bronze)
 4. The **legs** were of **iron**
 5. The **feet** of ten toes were a mixture of **iron** and **clay**.

vs.34-35   The Stone
 1. A stone was unnaturally cut out of a mountain.
 2. The stone smashed the image on it's feet and broke the ten toes.
 3. The whole image of **iron, clay, brass, silver and gold was broken into pieces and became like chaff** carried away by the wind and nothing could be found remaining of the image.
 4. **The stone that smashed the image became a great mountain and filled the whole earth.** This is a reference to the Battle of Armageddon and the thousand year reign of Christ on earth. *Rev. 19:17-21; 20:1-6*

But what did the dream mean? Daniel had given the king the dream. Could he also give the interpretation as he had spoken in faith to the king?

9. The Details

v.36 Having told the dream, Daniel moves right on to the interpretation of the dream.

The First World Empire: Babylon The Head of Gold

v.37 No mistake here. Daniel tells the king that he is *a king of kings* speaking of his dominion over nations and kings. *The God of heaven hath given thee a kingdom, power, and strength, and glory.*

v.38 *And wheresoever the children of men dwell, the beasts of the field and the fowls of the heaven hath he given into thine hand, and hath made thee ruler over them all.* The divine right to rule had been given him by God. The whole wording reveals the absolute sovereignty of God. Daniel then declares to the King Nebuchadnezzar "You are the *head of gold*".

The Golden City

Gold was its trade mark. Under Nebuchadnezzar, Babylon was the center of wealth and glory. Gold flowed into the city from all the provinces of the Babylonian Empire. The treasures of gold from Solomon's days in Jerusalem and onwards were all taken to Babylon. 90 years after the reign of Nebuchadnezzar, Herodotus the Greek Historian visited Babylon and he could not believe what he saw. He had never seen a city so full of gold. It was everywhere. The temples, alters, shrines, chapels, utensils were all plated with gold. Isa 14:4 refers to

Babylon as *the golden city*. Jeremiah says that *Babylon hath been a golden cup in the Lord's hand.* Jer.51:7

We need to remember that our salvation is not in riches but in Jesus Christ. Acts 4:12 He is the only Saviour. In Him there is peace, joy and the assurance of heaven when we die. 1 John 5:13

The Period of the Babylonian Empire 605 – 539 B.C.

The times of the Gentiles began with the captivity of Judah under Nebuchadnezzar and will end at the second coming of Christ.

v.39 Nebuchadnezzar's jurisdiction was the first organized one-worldwide Empire. It was soon to fall. Dan.5

The Second World Empire: Medo-Persia

And after thee (Nebuchadnezzar) *shall arise another kingdom inferior to thee.* We do not learn much about the Medo-Persian Empire from the image of Daniel in chapter 2. We learn more about this in chapters 5, 7, and 8. History shows that the next kingdom to come to power was Medo-Persian Empire. This was the 'arms and breast" of the image. It was the silver kingdom. It was indeed the inferior to the kingdom of Babylon, as silver is inferior to gold. Persian was known in history for her immense treasures and hoards of silver. Xerxes, a prominent King of Persia, inherited vast amounts of silver from his father, Darius Hystapes. History shows that in the Medo-Persia Empire all taxes had to be paid in sliver. The kingdom was to last about 200 years, approximate dates: 539-332 B.C. The two arms speak of a dual kingdom of the Medes (Darius) and Persians (Cyrus).

CHAPTER 2

The Third World Empire: Greece : 331-146 B.C.

And another third kingdom of brass, which shall rule over all the earth. The Military government of Greece was ruled by its first king - Alexander the Great. Alexander, the son of King Philip of Macedonia, shows signs of genius even when a teenager. His father obtained for him the best possible tutor, the great philosopher Aristotle. Alexander kept in touch with his teacher throughout all his military campaigns. By the time he was 25 he had the world at his feet. His life was characterized by drunken and licentious orgies and he died at 33 as the direct consequence of a debauch. In this empire there was further deterioration in government and the character of its rulers.

The Greeks were experts at molding brass. The soldiers wore breastplate of brass, helmet of brass and carried shields of brass, along with brass swords.

The marching armies were noted for their brass armour.

After Alexander's sudden death, the Grecian Empire was divided to his four generals. Fuller and further details will be dealt with when we get to chapters 7 and 8.

The Fourth World: Rome

v.40 The fourth Empire, Rome is not mentioned by name in Daniel. How do we know it is Rome? Turn to Luke 2:1 where we learn that the Roman Emperor Caesar Augustus was in control of the then known world.

Greece was succeeded by a fourth Gentile kingdom represented by the images legs of iron and feet and toes of iron and clay. This would be the Roman Empire. God's portrayal of Rome with two legs was very fitting, for the ancient Roman Empire ruled extensive areas of both the western and eastern division of the known world. In 395 A.D. the Roman Empire was divided politically into two divisions – the Western Roman Empire with Rome as its capital and the Eastern Roman Empire with Constantinople as its capital. (Constantinople's location is now Istanbul in the country Turkey.)

Iron was an excellent designation of Rome for at least two reasons.
- Ancient Rome was noted for its use of iron in its military weaponry.
- Just as Daniel indicated here; just as iron is able to crush gold, silver and bronze because it is stronger, so Rome would crush and shatter the ancient world. Ancient Rome did just that through it is great military strength. This aspect of the prophetic dream was fulfilled when Rome conquered Greece by 146 B.C. The Roman Empire ceased as a world power in 476 A.D. It will be brought to life again in the last days in the form of a ten nation confederation. *Dan.7:24; Rev.13:1-3; 17:12*

The Final Form of Gentile World Dominion vs.41-43

The Roman Empire would experience two distinct stages of an earlier (legs of iron) and latter (feet and ten toes) stage: part of potter's clay, part iron. The final stage of the Roman Empire would be strong military characterized by division. Different groups of people would combine with one another to form the final stage of the empire. But they would not submit one to another - just as iron and clay cannot combine completely together.
- **Iron speaks of strength**
- **Clay speaks of weakness**
- **The clay of the will is easily molded.**
- **This kingdom has for its foundation clay; it will not stand but fall.**

- The Roman Empires final stage consists of a ten Nation Confederation kingdom. *Dan.7:23-24; Rev.17:12*

The iron represented the ancient Roman Empire.

When was the feet and toe stage to exist?

There has never been a ten nation confederation in past history. Sometime beyond the present there will be a revival of a Roman Empire. I believe the ten toes represent this revival. This will be after the Church has been raptured to Heaven.

Fragments of the Roman Empire still exist today. One may travel to most European countries, and find magnificent buildings testifying to the great architectural and engineering skills of the Romans. Not only was Rome a glorious Empire 2000 years ago, but Roman Philosophy, Culture and Law are the foundation of virtually all western civilized nations. Her religion is still with us today: the Roman Catholic Church.

Decline and fall of the Roman Empire in the west lasted until 476 A.D. when it fell before invaders from the north. The Eastern Empire continued however until the fall of Constantinople in 1453 A.D.

The Final World Empire: the Kingdom of Heaven

v.44 *It is in the days of these* **ten** *kings that the God of Heaven* **will** *set up* **His** *kingdom.* The very wording gives us some identification of the 'time element' of events here. The kingdom of ten toes (10 kings) must be in existence when Christ comes again.

v.45   The Stone

It is *cut out of the mountain without hands.* No human hand did this. It was God. It was supernatural and an everlasting kingdom. This is the Millennial kingdom, the thousand year reign of Jesus Christ. *Rev.20:1-6*
The stone therefore smites the image on the ten toes *v.34* for that is the kingdom in existence when Christ comes the second time. *Rev.19:11-21* Although the stone hits the feet, the whole of the image is crushed to powder.
The feet are the end of the body, and this kingdom is the end of the world kingdoms. That spirit which was evident in 'the head' goes 'through the body' to 'the feet' and is judged accordingly by Christ.

10. The Declaration of Nebuchadnezzar

vs.46-49

The king, overwhelmed with the revelation of the dream and interpretation, *fell upon his face, and worshipped Daniel.* He commanded that *an oblation* (an offering) *and sweet odours* be offered to Daniel. One could rest assured that Daniel would not accept such idolatrous honor, which belongs to God only. However, Daniel would know that the king really knew no better, as a heather idolater. He could accept the king's honor without the idolatry.

v.47 Nebuchadnezzar still calls Daniel's God *your God*, not yet being humbled as in chapter 4. I personally believe that God was softening Nebuchadnezzar's heart.

v.48-49   Daniel and his three friends (Daniel did not forget his three friends) are now promoted to important

CHAPTER 2

places in the kingdom *for them that honour me I will honour.* 1 Sam.2:30; Ps.75:6-7

Chapter 3

The Image and the Furnace

1. The Pride and Willfulness of the King

v.1   The Glory of Man

....the king made an image of gold. The king in his vanity and pride now sets up, not a head of gold, but a complete statue of gold for the people to worship. God gave Nebuchadnezzar power to rule, but he used it to glorify himself; to deny the true God; and to force men to worship his false gods.

- If a cubit is 18 inches, the image was 90 feet high and 9 feet wide -.

The plain of Dura was flat and expansive, enabling a great multitude to assemble to worship the image.

The number six in Scripture is significant of beast and man. Gen.1:24-23 shows that beasts and man were created on the sixth day; thus the number six is stamped upon beast and man. The significance of this is seen in chapter 3 where the king of Babylon sets up an image of idolatry, impressed with the number six and because of his pride, in chapter 4 he is the man who becomes like a beast! All, of course, points to Revelation 13 where the Antichrist is a man who becomes the Beast! It is the False Prophet who would cause all to worship his image and take his mark, number or name: 666. Number 6 is man's number, the number of failure.

Number 7 is God's Divine number of Divine perfection. Man never quite gets there: he comes short.

CHAPTER 3

v.2 The Government Officials
The Unification of Religion
Nebuchadnezzar understood the best way to unite people politically is to unite them religiously. The king decreed that all the nobles of his empire were to gather together for *the dedication of* his golden *image.* Generally speaking, we can say that all civil, military, and judicial high dignitaries were present. This was more than a political assembly; it was a religious service. [Note: the word 'worship' is used at least 9 times in this chapter.] It appears that this was an effort to unify all the religions of the earth, and his Empire to worship himself – much as the Antichrist will do. *2 Thes.2:3-11; Rev.13:1-18* Religion, the king reasoned, must be made subservient (or useful) to political aims. The Devil could not accomplish his plan if there were no earthly religions.

2. The Proclamation to Worship by the King

Nebuchadnezzar probably stood before the image to receive their worship and adoration.

v.3 A Powerful Order Obeyed
This verse affirms that all the rulers of the providence of Nebuchadnezzar Empire came at his call, and stood before the monstrous golden image to admire and worship it. It simply added to the dead gods they already worshiped. *Ps.115:4-9; Mt.7:13; Rom.1:21-28*

vs.4-5 A Paid Orator
The king's herald announced with a loud voice what Nebuchadnezzar commanded. All the people must **fall down together and worship the golden image** when they heard the sound of music. It was loud and clear.

v.6 They had to 'toe the party line' and bow down to the golden image. Failure to do so would mean being thrown into **a burning fiery furnace**. It was 'pay homage or else'....prostration – or extermination!

v.7   A Pathetic (sad moving) Ordeal

Beware of the charm of today's modern music. Music got off to a bad start – mentioned first in the godless line of Cain. *Gen.4:21* When music or ritual appeals to the flesh it degrades man rather than elevates him, and does not glorify God.

There are six musical instruments listed *vs.5, 7*
1. **Corne**t – a wood wind instrument
2. **Flute** – a wind instrument
3. **Harp** – a string instrument
4. **Sackbut** – a trombone, or high stringed instrument
5. **Psaltery** – a string instrument like a Harp
6. **Dulcimer** – a drum with strings above, played with a stick.

'and all kinds of music' indicating that not all the instruments and types of music are mentioned.

Music that is Spiritual is a wonderful aid to glorify and worship God. Paul shows the importance of music in church worship. *Eph.5:19; Col.3:16*

The fear of this fire turned men to the image, but the fear of eternal fire does not turn many to Christ; the love of Christ, in delivering from the wrath to come, is accepted only by the minority.

CHAPTER 3

3. The Personal Witness of the Three Hebrews

The Dismay of the Majority

vs.8-12   The Watchers

In the middle of this mass idolatrous worship scene, some of the Chaldeans were watching. They would already know of Daniel, Shadrach, Meshach, and Abed-nego who had 'their own God" and were not given to the worship of other gods. They saw what they expected; three of these men did not bow to the king's image. Shadrach, Meshach and Abed-nego were swimming against the tide. They did not go with the crowd. They stood their ground. They were not prepared to sell their birthright. Their principles were not up for sale; they had different set of values. It will cost us when we take a stand for God. Even Paul's familiar friends forsook him. *2 Tim.4:16*

v.13-15   The Warning

Surrounded by an angry mob they were easy prey for the more militant in the company. The agitators were keen to whip up the frenzy of the violent multitude. Within minutes they were denounced in the presence of the king by a handful of astrologers. They were bent on revenge; an ill wind was blowing. A conspiracy was being planned and a plot was hatched to get rid of them.

A threefold charge was made against them
- They **disregarded** the sovereign – this lack of personal respect for the king.
- They **disobeyed** the statement – non-conformity to the kings worship.
- They **disapproved** of the statue – according to the king this was rebellion, anarchy.

vs.16-18   The Witness

In response to the *'that God'* statement made by Nebuchadnezzar in v.15, they finally replied: *'Our God'*. Consider their answer.
1. ***Our God whom we serve is able to deliver us from the burning fiery furnace***. They expressed their faith in God's ability. Our God is able.
2. Our God is able to ***deliver us out of thine hand, O king.*** God is willing.
3. ***But if not*** – we will not bow or serve your gods.
4. We will not bow down ***nor worship the golden image which thou hast set up.***

There is nothing of disrespect here. There is nothing of compromise. They would not yield to any pressure of the king, or peer pressure of public pressure, music or power pressure. They were willing to stand alone in the face of death.

The Sovereignty of God

There is something of the sovereignty of God evidenced here in their confession of faith.

Sovereignty is that which is super, above, superior to all, chief, supreme in power, original authority and jurisdiction. This is one of the great attributes of God. He is over all. He had the right to exercise any right and power over His creatures, as He wills. God being who He is can do what He likes and how He likes. His will is good, perfect and acceptable to those who trust Him. *Rom.12:1-2*

This is what is seen in the sovereignty of God. God is under no obligation and cannot be pressured by human pressure or presumption. God says...***For my thoughts are not your thoughts, neither are your ways my***

ways. . .For as the heavens are higher than the earth, so are my ways higher than your ways, and my thoughts than your thoughts. Isa.55:8-9
In Isaiah 55, the gospel invitation is to the Jew and Gentile: The restoration of Israel back to the Holy Land, and the Millennium Reign of Christ. These words in vs.8-9 are richly applied to all time and circumstances.

4. The Preservation and Welfare of the Three Hebrews

Freedom in the Fire
        1. They would not **Bow**...
        2. They would not **Budge**...
        3. They would not **Bend**...
        4. They would not **Burn**...

The Madness of the Monarch

v.19 The three young men stand before the king unflinching and unyielding. He changes color as his anger reaches boiling point. He had been humiliated by three Jews and that was more than he was prepared to take. The fire was raging in the furnace as he signaled to the stoker to switch up the temperature *seven times* hotter.

v.20 His mighty men were commanded to bind Shadrach, Meshach, and Abed-nego and hurl them into the inferno.

v.21 Without any offer of resistance, the three complied with the death sentence that had been handed down.

The Magnitude of the Miraculous

v.22

The furnace probably resembled a modern day limekiln with an opening in the top for the flames and smoke and another opening at ground level for stoking the fire. The mighty men carried the three Hebrews and tossed them into the excessive heat. Before the mighty men could retreat – they were burned alive! It was like an incinerator for them on the outside as they went up in smoke.

What must it been like on the inside? God allows us to go through the fire of affliction so that our enemies might be destroyed.
    We have enemies:
- Pride
- Selfishness
- self-desire
- evil
- deceit
- uncleanness
- worldliness
- carnality

    all of these are our enemies.

v.23 *Shadrach, Meshach, and Abed-nego, fell down bound into the midst of the burning fiery furnace.* It brought them low, they fell down. God allows us to go through the 'fire of affliction' that it might bring us low. In times of tribulation we realize our helplessness. Just as Shadrach, Meshach and Abed-nego were brought down so God allows you and me to go through the refining fire that we might learn lowliness; that we might learn to be humble. Paul says....*God, that comforteth those that*

CHAPTER 3

are cast down. 2 Cor. 7:6 The word *cast down* means 'brought low'.

v.24 Nebuchadnezzar can't resist the temptation to get the last laugh. He looks through the furnace door and the shock is almost too much for him. He is baffled and bewildered. He suffered a momentary lapse of concentration as he tried to reconcile what he saw with what he knew was true; three were thrown into the furnace. But he saw four.......

The Mystery Man

v.25 The fourth man was the Son of God; the pre-incarnate Christ. Nebuchadnezzar not having spiritual perception could only testify to his unusual appearance. The three Hebrew found liberty in the flames as they were bound. They found freedom in the fire as they were able to walk around. Isaiah prophesied...*When thou passest through the waters, I will be with thee; and through the rivers, they shall not overflow thee: when thou walkest through the fire, thou shalt not be burned; neither shall the flame kindle upon thee.* Isa.43:2

In addition to the three Hebrews, Nebuchadnezzar also saw a divine figure in the furnace: The Son of God. Whenever His children are in the fiery furnace of trials for His name sake, He is there. Christ never sends forth His sheep unless He goes on before them.

v.26 Nebuchadnezzar calls Shadrach, Meshach and Abed-nego to come forth out of the fiery furnace.

v.27 They came out triumphant. They were unmarked. They were unharmed.
        No Scars
                No Sores

> No Smell
> Nothing was Singed.

God had undertaken for them.

The Musing of the Monarch

v.28 The king, though not yet evidencing personal faith in the Lord, is completely impressed.

v.29 He warns against anyone speaking anything amiss about the God of these three Hebrew boys. But he must be further humbled before he makes real acknowledgment of the God of Heaven in relation to himself. In chapter 4 we hear his personal testimony of his conversion.

v.30 Promotion to higher office was the outcome for Shadrach, Meshach and Abed-nego. All is well that ends well. For them, and it can be for each of us, a journey from trial to triumph. Man's extremity is often God's opportunity. It shows beyond any shadow of doubt that when we are at the end of ourselves - we are only at the beginning of God.

Who through faith . . .Quenched the violence of fire.
Heb.11:33-34

Chapter 4

1. The Regenerate King Speaks

1. Nebuchadnezzar Testimony

The testimony of Nebuchadnezzar belongs chronologically at the conclusion of the chapter. His statement grows out of the experiences recorded in verses 4-33. In these verses is what the king experienced **before** his conversion.

v.1 Now Nebuchadnezzar wants the world to know what God had done for Him. He speaks to:
- All People
- Nations
- Languages
- All the Earth

His Desire

Peace be multiplied unto you. The king longed in his heart that others that did not know God might have that peace which he had experienced.

v.2 His Declaration

As Nebuchadnezzar begins his word of testimony, he is baffled and overwhelmed by the glory of God.
I thought it good to shew the signs and wonders that the high God hath wrought toward me.
Then you would expect him to tell you all about the signs and wonders; but floods of overwhelming joy filled his soul and what he says is just exclamations. He said the greatness was beyond his ability to understand. He was overwhelmed at God's grace and mercy which had reached down and saved a wretch like him.

v.3 His Devotion

How great are his signs! and how mighty are his wonders! We find the same overwhelming inability to describe religious experience in the Apostle Paul. After Paul struggles through Romans 9-11 to describe the sovereignty and the elective purpose of God, he just ends in an exclamation. He cannot say more.
O the depth of the riches both of the wisdom and knowledge of God! how unsearchable are his judgments, and his ways past finding out! Rom.11:33

Nebuchadnezzar contrasted God's rule to his own. God's rule is eternal and does not change, whereas Nebuchadnezzar's had been the opposite.

2. The Relating of the Dream

v.4 The Prosperous King

At the start of his narrative, the king described his situation and stated that he was both 'secure' and prospering. Nebuchadnezzar was both self-centered and self-satisfied. Matthew 16:26 says *For what is a man profited, if he shall gain the whole world, and lose his own soul? or what shall a man give in exchange for his soul?*
'*at rest*' : 'at ease'; not indicating resting in sleep but an expression of contentment, security and prosperity. However, it was a false sense of security.

v.5 The Dream of the King

I saw a dream..... This is the second dream God gave the king. God speaks once, then twice in order to draw men away from their pride; so says Job 33:14-17. Note the

CHAPTER 4

pride of the king in Daniel 4:23,24,29,30. But dreams, especially from God, need to be interpreted. God had such a man: Daniel. The Psalmist says ***God hath spoken once; twice have I heard this; that power belongeth unto God.*** Ps.62:11

The Disturbed King
. . .which made me afraid, The Hebrew word 'afraid' means: make afraid, fear, dreadful, terrible. The Hebrew word 'trouble' means 'to terrify'. Nebuchadnezzar became extremely afraid. As happened earlier in Daniel 2:1, the king saw a dream that greatly disturbed him. That was its purpose.

vs.6-7   The Professional Group
The king went to the wrong source. It is always natural for one to seek help on his own level rather that turn to God; human nature remains unchanged. But these wise men were helpless to explain the dream as well.

vs.8-9   The Proposition is Put to Daniel
The question arises as to why Daniel was not called in at the first. Perhaps, as still a pagan, the king was once again relying on the wisdom of men, and delayed turning to the man of God as he had done 33 years earlier. Nebuchadnezzar referred to Daniel as 'Chief of the Magicians', one who could explain the mysteries that confused everyone else.
To him the living God of Daniel was just another god in his realm. Notice that he said, in whom ***the spirit of the holy gods is***. The king continued to think like a heathen.

vs.10-12   The Provision

Below – the **Features of the Tree** will be on the left and the **_Symbolic Meaning_** will be in italics and indented to the right.

The *tree* v.10
> *The king himself v.22*

In the midst of the earth v.10
> *The Babylonian Empire so vitally linked with Nebuchadnezzar its king, radiated its power throughout the habitable world from a central position on the earth.*

Great in height and reaching to heaven vs.10-11
> *Nebuchadnezzar was the undisputed ruler of nations at that time.*

The tree grew, and was strong v.11
> *The prosperity and strength of Babylon was established.*

The tree was visible from a great distance v.11
> *The influence of the Babylonian Empire was global.*

The leaves were fair (beautiful) v.12
> *The magnificence and breathtaking beauty of Babylon was unparallel.*

The abundance of fruit was food for all v.12
> *The intention of God was that the great empires of earth should be for the benefit of mankind providing food, shelter, rest, and security.*

CHAPTER 4

Provided shade and shelter for the beasts of the field
v.12
> *A tree provides fuel, food, furniture, building material, decoration and shade.*

The birds of the air nested in its branches *v.12*
All flesh was fed. *v.12*
> It is on record in one of his inscriptions concerning his great empire 'Under her everlasting shadow I gather all men in peace. Vast heaps of grain beyond measure I store up within her'

v.13   The Participant

"*watcher*" and "*holy one*" are an order of created intelligences (angels). The watchers are the holy ones who administer the affairs of this world. They see all, they hear all, and they tell all. The Christian is constantly under the eye of God. *Ps.139:11-12* Angels do come down from heaven, as watchful ministers to do God's will among men, in blessing the righteous and judging or smiting the wicked at the bidding of the Lord even still. *Ps.34:7; 103:20-21; Heb.1:14; Dan.10:13-21.* We are not to worship angels. They cannot save us, only Jesus can save us from our sins. *Matt.1:21; Acts 4:12; Rev.22:8-9*

v.14   The Power

He cried aloud... 'with might, as of a herald'. This scene is one of desolation though not annihilation. Though the Babylonian Empire was later cut down, the city itself was not destroyed. However, the dream is primarily to do with Nebuchadnezzar, for the period of time of his insanity, his kingdom was preserved.

The implication is one of warning before judgment, a principle of Divine justice in judgment. *Mt.3:10; Lk.13:6-9* For such calls of judgment consider Rev.14:15-20 and Ezekiel 31:1. Egypt's downfall compared to Assyria's collapse. God is warning America – Are we listening?

v.15 The Prospect

Nevertheless leave the stump. The prospect of Nebuchadnezzar being restored; the tree was not completely uprooted. Also this was symbolic of the disciplining of Nebuchadnezzar, but not his destruction.

A band of iron and brass... Doubtless this was to keep the stump from splitting, spreading and dying. Keeping it moist would also keep it from dying out under the intense heat of the day.

v.16 The Period of Time

The heart of the king is changed to the heart of a beast. This strange condition is to last for a period of ***seven times*** (or seven years). This period is also mentioned in verses 23, 25, 32. The fact that 'a time' means one year is seen in Revelation, where we read of the identity of three and one-half years as
- ***forty and two months*** *Rev.11:2*
- ***a thousand two hundred and threescore days*** *Rev.12:6*
- ***a time, and times, and half a time*** *Rev.12:14*

v.17 The Preeminence of God

Decree
Not the same word as the king's decree in 2:9 (Royal decree, Law) or in 3:10 (Commandment) but rather the sentence that determines the fate of any person. *(F.C. Cook)*

CHAPTER 4

Demand ....of the Holy Ones
The holy ones as administrators and executors of the divine will of God. It seems that the lone watcher of v.13 reported back to the council chambers of Heaven. The holy angels, so sensitive to the divine will of God and anxious to carry it out to the letter, took council together and made decisions accordingly.

The most High
That is the Almighty God. It is He that ruleth in the kingdom of men. (Frail mortal men.)

The Basest of Men
The Lowest of men; the lowliest in rank and esteem. They can be good or evil. History reveals that Nebuchadnezzar was of humble origin. His father King Nabopolassar was not of royal birth but came of unknown parentage.

There is a remarkable passage in the prophecy recorded in Jeremiah concerning Nebuchadnezzar
 I have made the earth, the man and the beast that are upon the ground, by my great power and by my outstretched arm, and have given it unto whom it seemed meet unto me. And now have I given all these lands into the hand of Nebuchadnezzar the King of Babylon, my servant; and the beasts of the field have I given him also to serve him. And all nations shall serve him, and his son, and his son's son, until the very time of his land come: and then many nations and great kings shall serve themselves of him. And it shall come to pass, that the nation and kingdom which will not serve the same Nebuchadnezzar the King of Babylon, and that will not put their neck under the yoke of the King of Babylon, that nation will I

punish, saith the Lord, with the sword, and with the famine, and with the pestilence, until I have consumed them by his hand. Jer.27:5-8

Nebuchadnezzar was a great and mighty king, God called him ***my servant***. Jer.25:9; 27:6 Even though he was still unconverted at this time. How solemn the realization that the fall of Nebuchadnezzar was because of his pride and at the request of the angelic administrators.

v.18   The Powerless *Wise Men*
The wise men could not help the king. Daniel waited until he was called. The king needed spiritual help, and the false pretenders of wisdom understood not the dream.

3. The Revelation of the Dream

v.19   The Astonishment of Daniel
Daniel was so ***astonished*** that he could not speak ***for one hour***. He wished that the meaning of the dream could be for the king's enemies – and not the king himself.

The Assessment of Daniel
vs.20-21   First he described the tree in its glory, using almost the same words as in verses 10-12. This shows that Daniel paid close attention to what the king said and remembered it very well.

vs.22-23   The tree was a picture of Nebuchadnezzar, who had become strong and great and who ruled over many countries and influenced all others. But the rest of the dream must also mean Nebuchadnezzar. Here Daniel did not repeat all the details of the judgment. He said the

CHAPTER 4

command was to cut down the tree but leave the stump and the roots in the field. The king would be with the animals for seven periods of time (seven years)

vs.24-25   Daniel knew that the angels were just doing the will of God, and the command really came from the most High. The king would live with the animals, eat grass like an ox, and be exposed to the weather for seven periods of time.

v.26   Nebuchadnezzar would have to learn that God rules over men and He is supreme.

v.27   The Appeal of Daniel

Wherefore, O king – The king had not asked him for any advice of favour. Daniel goes further and gives counsel to the king he loved. He sees the judgment of God, and yet he said "it may be deferred, may be averted". "I know that His mercies are great, and as one who loves you – know that two things are necessary". First repent of your sins, second "bring forth fruit meet for repentance." To turn to the Lord **and shew mercy to the poor** Daniel assured him, might be a means of lengthening the days of tranquility (prosperity) on earth. *Ps.41:1*

Sin is a galling yoke; a burden for a sinner to bear. He need not bear it, if he will turn to the Lord. Such as Daniel's plea to this heathen Gentile one-world Ruler.

Hezekiah turned, his days were lengthened. *Isa.38:1-5*
Nineveh repented, and the city was spared. *Jonah 3:5-10; Jer.18:7-8*

4. The Rebellion of Nebuchadnezzar

The Accomplishments of Nebuchadnezzar

Nebuchadnezzar ruled a great empire Babylonia. He also rebuilt and beautified Babylon until it was the most magnificent city this world had ever seen. The king soon forgot the faithful warning of Daniel. All that he predicted was fulfilled in the life of King Nebuchadnezzar.

vs.28-29   Procrastination

God in His grace and mercy gave Nebuchadnezzar 12 months to come to repentance. This period is likened to '*space to repent*'. *Rev.2:21*

God gives to all mankind 'space' or 'time to repent'. It is like walking a path. No one knows how long that pathway may be - but when one comes to the end of that pathway, if there is no repentance, then the judgment of God falls. The judgments of God are slow but sure. The king continued along the pathway of his own destiny without repentance. At the end of this 'space' (12 months) God was there in judgment.

If you have not done so - turn now while there is time; come to Jesus, ask Him to save you. *For whosoever shall call upon the name of the Lord shall be saved*. *Rom.10:13*

v.30   Pride

Pride brings shame. *Prov.11:2* *Pride goeth before destruction, and an haughty spirit before a fall*. *Prov.16:18* This statement of the king was saturated with pride and conceit. He was obsessed with his greatness of his achievements, seemingly at the expense of attending to the needs 'of the poor' v.27.

v.31.a   The Proclamation
there fell a voice from heaven. No matter how great a man might be, he cannot avert the ultimate judgment of God.

5. The Retribution of God

v.31.b   The Announcement from Heaven
The kingdom is departed from thee. All connection with God was lost. The clock of judgment has struck in Heaven. Judgment falls upon this man whose arrogant pride has stripped him. God deals with him personally. The insane of that day were driven out rather than being placed in an institution.

vs.32-33   The Animal-like Characteristic
When men reject the Word of God they sink to the level of beasts. Man is not the descendent of the beast, but he lives like an animal today when he leaves out God and rejects His Word.

    Edward Dennet writes in his book "*Daniel the Prophet*" "when a man in his exaltation shuts out God from his thoughts, and makes himself the centre and object, he is morally no better than a beast."

6. The Restoration

v.34 The Salvation of God
In vs.28-33 the king looked at Babylon.
In vs.34-37 he looks up to heaven.

The Scripture says **Look unto me, and be ye saved, all the ends of the earth: for I am God, and there is none else**. *Isa.45:22* King Nebuchadnezzar is a wise man at last. The vision is no longer filled with self; but he is gazing up to glory.

End of Days. This is a reference to the end of the predicted period of seven years. Nebuchadnezzar first lifted up his eyes to Heaven and then he experienced the return of his understanding. Then as he looks up to Heaven he learns the ways of God. What about his glory now? He has no time to bother with that, no time to think of <u>his</u> glory;

This is the perfect antidote for the sin of pride.
1. ***I blessed the most High,***
2. ***and I praised and honoured him that liveth for ever,***
3. ***whose dominion is an everlasting dominion, and***
4. ***his kingdom is from generation to generation:***

It is good when we keep our eyes looking Heaven-ward, with understanding. The salvation of God delivered Nebuchadnezzar from sins penalty and himself.

v.35 The Sovereignty of God
and he doeth according to his will

CHAPTER 4

Being the Lord of Hosts, and the only absolute and universal Monarch of the world; ***None can stay his hand, or say unto him, What doest thou?*** He is irresistible and uncontrollable. None can prevent His will being accomplished, nor can they question it directly to His face.

v.36 The Seeking Counselors and Lords
Nebuchadnezzar's mind returned; and his counselors to help him again. They gave him honor and majesty as before, and even more.

v.37 The Satisfaction of Nebuchadnezzar
Nebuchadnezzar finishes his testimony with the dealings of God with him before his conversion.

1. *Praise* – to pronounce Happy
   He surely had been brought to a blessed and happy state.
2. *Extol* – Lift up
   The God that he once rebelled against, now he lifts up, and exalts.
3. *Honour* - glorious
   Now that God is Nebuchadnezzar's personal Saviour – he honors, glorifies His name.
4. *The King of Heaven*
   God is recognized. ***The King of Heaven*** because everything He does is right.
5. *All whose works are truth*
   God's works are in harmony with His truth.

   God's works are described as
   - *Terrible* Ps. 66:3
   - *Incomparable* Ps. 86:8

- **Great** *Ps.92:5*
- **Manifold** *Ps.104:24*
- **Marvelous** *Ps.139:14*

God's Word as
- **Truth** *Jn.17:17 thy word is truth.*

- **Book of Ages** *Ps.119:89* <u>**For ever**</u>, *O Lord, thy word is settled in heaven.*
- **Divinely Inspired** *Jer.36:2; Eze.1:3; 2 Tim.3:16; 2 Pet.1:21; Rev.14:13*
- **Furnishes a Light** *Ps.19:8; 119:105 119.130; 2 Pet.1:19*
- **Despised by the foolish** *Isa.5:24; 30:12; 2 Chr.36:16; Mk.7:9*
- **Loved by the saints** *Ps.119:47, 97, 140*

6. And his ways judgment

The righteous judgment and fairness of God dealings with him are freely acknowledged to the whole world. For God is faithful to His promise and just in His dealings.

7. God Subdues the Proud
and those that walk in pride he is able to abase.

God will not allow our pride or egotism to go unchecked. He will use extreme pain, sickness or hardship to remove ingratitude from our lives so that we will acknowledge our dependence on Him. That Nebuchadnezzar trusted the only God who could deliver him from his sin of pride and restore him physically, mentally, and spiritually.

The king trusted in
- the Scriptural God (the Son of God)
- by Scriptural Means (Faith)

CHAPTER 4

- for the Scriptural Work (Deliverance from sin)
- to receive the Scriptural Future (His eternal Kingdom)

Chapter 5

Belshazzar was the King of Babylon, but his father Nabonidus was still living. Old books of history tell us that Nabonidus was away from home several years and he appointed his son Belshazzar to rule as king while he was out of Babylon.

As to the matter of the father-son relationship between Nebuchadnezzar and Belshazzar mentioned in Daniel 5 – there is no real problem. Bible scholar R.D. Wilson has shown that among the Arabs and Babylonians the word 'son' was used in not less than twelve ways, including 'grandson' and 'adopted son'; and the word 'father' had no fewer than seven different uses. The word 'father' was used for any ancestor, for one's Father, Grandfather, Great-Grandfather, 2nd Great-Grandfather – and even back beyond that. Tablet and clay cylinders have been discovered in the ruins of Chaldea on which the name Belshazzar was inscribed as the eldest son of Nabonidus.

1. Belshazzar's Feast

Deception – Drunkenness

v.1   Belshazzar was deceived by strong drink.
Wine is a mocker, strong drink is raging: and whosoever is deceived thereby is not wise. Prov.20:1 *It is not for kings, O Lemuel, it is not for kings to drink wine; nor for princes strong drink: Lest they drink, and forget the law, and pervert the judgment of any of the afflicted.* Prov.31:4-5

CHAPTER 5

If the student of the Bible has been disappointed in the conduct of Presidents, Prime Ministers, or Heads of State during the "Times of the Gentiles", he has not reached the end of the sad story. Their usual pattern is to first commit idolatry and defy God's claims on their individual consciences. Next they usually become insane in their pride, and they fail to recognize the authority of God in worldly affairs.

vs.2-3   The Defilers

Things got out of hand. It snowballed as they engage in noisy acts of desecration towards the vessels that Nebuchadnezzar brought from the Temple in Jerusalem. It was sacrilege. It was an act of open defiance and sheer contempt. Profanity was in the air. Women in the East were always in strict isolation. But not here! In the presence of men unable to control their passions and incapable of answering for their actions because of drunkenness you can imagine what was happening. Morality went out the window and dissipated within hours.

In times of drunkenness men and women stoop to do things they would not do while sober. The only reason women would be in attendance at a party like this would be for immoral purposes. That's the problem with worldly parties.

v.4   The Depraved

This was the crowning insult to God – they veiled their blasphemy in the name of religion. They covered their sin as an act of worship. Significantly six of their gods are named: gold, silver, brass, iron, wood, stone. 'Six' is the world's number destined for judgment and hostile to God.

There are more gods in Japan than there are Japanese to worship them. There is at least 300 million gods in India.

God is *longsuffering; great in mercy and slow to anger;* Ps.86:5; 103:8; 145:8 *not willing that any should perish, but that all should come to repentance.* 2 Pet.3:9

When Belshazzar and his guests poured wine into the sacred vessels, and lifted those vessels to their drunken lips, the cup of iniquity for Babylon was filled to the brim! The second Belshazzar stepped across God's deadline he plunged into eternal darkness and doom.

2. Belshazzar's Fear

The Fingers

v.5 *In the same hour* . . .God appeared in the form of the *fingers of a man's hand.* Just the writing fingers, as they wrote on the plaster of that huge festival hall, above the candlesticks, where it was clearly visible to King Belshazzar - the king saw the part of the hand that wrote. God warned Belshazzar not by a dream or a vision as he had Nebuchadnezzar, but the 'writing fingers". God draws the line. This is it; no further! The fingers writing doom and death.

The Fear

v.6 relates that the *king's countenance was changed*. His bright look turned ashen gray. His conscious *thoughts troubled him*, shook him up within, so that the joints, his vertebrae or backbone of his loins loosed. He becomes so weak with fear that he could hardly stand on his feet. So loose were his joints and weak were his knees that they '*smote one against another*"; knocked together. The discipline and the judgments of God are not pleasant.

v.7 continues that when Belshazzar regained his composure he cried aloud for the wise men to come to his aid. He offered a handsome reward. Besides rich gifts, the interpreter of the handwriting would be made **third ruler of the kingdom** – not the second. This is another example of the accurate details of this Book. Belshazzar, who was ruling **with** his father, was second in line: he could only offer **third** place.

The Failure
v.8   Powerless wise men
Though designated as wise men they were in reality useless and fraudulent. Though the letters of the writing were in Chaldean language, the wise men could not read them. Therefore their interpretation was impossible. God had reserved the privilege for His servant Daniel.

v.9   the Perplexed wise Men
If the king was troubled at the writing in v.6 now he is **greatly troubled**. *i.e.* Greatly alarmed because his wise men could not help him.

Belshazzar seems to have had a forewarning of the coming doom which was hidden in the writing. He is at his wit's end – not knowing where to turn in his dire need. He has exhausted all human resources. His Lords were astonished (perplexed) not only at the handwriting but at the change in Belshazzar. Belshazzar and his wise men were soon to learn that they were approaching their destruction.

The Faithful
v.10 Remembrance
It is evident that the queen (probably Nebuchadnezzar's wife) was not at the party. She would be older in years and possibly had no interest in such a festival, knowing what it would be like. It is evident also that she still remembered the dealings of God in her husband's life in the past years.

v.11 She also remembered Daniel's part in the interpretation of Nebuchadnezzar's dreams. During the reign of Belshazzar Daniel had evidently been forgotten. He was probably set aside by the pleasure-loving lustful Lords.

At this point, Daniel had been out of the public eye for twenty years. He was approximately 89 years old. Sometimes if God hasn't used us today, this week, or this month, we panic. Remember Romans 8:28 *and we know that all things work together for good to them that love God*. We need to remember that we are simply tools in the Lord's toolbox and He can pull us out whenever He wants to accomplish whatever He desires. Our job is simply to be ready, available, and open.

v.12 Recommendation
When the queen walks into the banquet house she quickly got down to business. She recommends that Belshazzar invite Daniel to solve the mystery (the writing on the wall). She had fond recollections of what Daniel did for her late husband, Nebuchadnezzar. Perhaps she too may have felt the same power. Who knows?

The Queen's evaluation of Daniel

She points out that there was found in Daniel:
The spirit of the holy gods. *v.11*. The queen knew something was different about Daniel. She wasn't versed enough in theology to say it was the Holy Spirit of God, but she recognized there was a different spirit in Daniel.

- **light** *v.11* Enlightenment
- **understanding** *v.11* Insight
- **wisdom** *v.11* Intelligent, skilful, or artful
- **excellent spirit** *v.12* Superb ability, preeminent, to abound to be over and above
- **knowdedge** *v.12* Skilled in understanding the time, to discern
- **understanding** *v.12* Insight
- **interpreting of dreams**
- **shewing of hard sentences**
- **dissolving of doubts** – or meaning ' Loosing of knots'; 'Solutions to problems'. The word 'doubts' is the same word as 'joints' in v.6

She recommended him as a person who could solve the most complex and difficult problems. That was a glorious testimony regarding Daniel before such a great multitude. At the right time God had His man ready.

3. Belshazzar's Failure

v.13 The Requirement

The king required the prophet to affirm his identity as Daniel, indicating that he did not recognize him, even though Daniel had previously been in his service. *Dan.8:1-27* The king also knew something about Daniel that the queen did not reveal, namely that he was a Jewish deportee. This no doubt irritated Belshazzar's concern for the message, since the messenger Daniel was from the same land (Judah) as the sacred vessels. These sacred vessels were used in the Temple in Jerusalem and were brought to Babylon by his grandfather Nebuchadnezzar.

v.14 The Recollection
The king now repeated the queen's recommendation of Daniel. Belshazzar did not describe the gods as 'holy gods' as Nebuchadnezzar and the queen had done. The word 'holy' uniquely describes Jehovah God. But the king's knowledge of the God of Daniel was limited and not from his own experience. Holiness was not associated with heathen gods.
Though Belshazzar did not know God, he did know what had befallen his grandfather at the hand of God.

v.15 The Readily Confession
Belshazzar readily confessed the failure of the wise men and astrologers. They were not able to read or explain the writing on the wall. **But the natural man receiveth not the things of the Spirit of God: for they are foolishness unto him: neither can he know them, because they are spiritually discerned.** 1 Cor. 2:14
Therefore we must beware of the theological utterances of unbelieving men, and of translations of the Scriptures by unbelieving scholars.

v.16 The Reward
The king offers to promote Daniel to the third highest in the kingdom if he can interpret the writing. ("Third ruler' means that Daniel would stand third in the chain of command under Belshazzar and another man.)

CHAPTER 5

v.17 The Refusal
Hearing of the reward, Daniel said 'I am not in this for the money, so keep your gifts, or give them to another. But I will tell you the meaning of this handwriting.

v.18 The Review
Daniel told Belshazzar about God, *the most High God*, who *gave Nebuchadnezzar*
> his *kingdom*
> his *majesty*
> his *glory*
> his *honour*

v.19 People of all nations feared Nebuchadnezzar, who had the power to kill anyone who opposed him - or to let him live; to give anyone a higher position or a lower one.

v.20 The glory and power made Nebuchadnezzar proud - and he lost his mind and his throne and all his glory.

v.21 He could not live with people, his heart was like the heart of a beast and he lived with the wild donkeys. He ate grass like an ox and his body was wet every night with dew, because he had no protection. This lasted seven years, un*til he knew that God most High* rules over men and kingdoms. God is Supreme; He gives authority to the person He chooses.

v.22 The Rebuke
Daniel rebuked the king for his sin of pride. Daniel added that Belshazzar knew about his Grandfather's sin, his insanity, and final restoration to the glory of God.

v.23 He charged the king with willful, deliberate blasphemy against God and desecration of the sacred vessels. His pride was **against the Lord of heaven** as the king and his nobles and their respective wives exalted the Babylonian gods above the most High God. They **praised the gods of silver, gold, brass, iron, wood, and stone**; they used the very breath which comes because of the grace of God, to praise the false gods and blaspheme God's Holy Name. The king deliberately refused to glorify God with his breath or his ways, and he fell under the judgment of God; God, who is Creator and Sovereign, sent as judge that part of the hand which wrote the mysterious message.

v.24   The Revelation
Thus the God whom Belshazzar had ignored wrote His startling message to the king on the wall of his own Palace. The divine communication could not have been more direct, and not for one moment did Belshazzar doubt that it was meant for him.

v.25 *And this is the writing that was written, MENE, MENE, TEKEL, UPHARSIN.*

v.26 *Mene* means 'numbered'. Why would he repeat that word? It means he hath numbered – he hath numbered – emphasized with absolute certainty that the king's days were numbered; also the Babylonian Empire. Both were finished.

v.27   *Tekel* means 'weighed'. God had weighed Belshazzar on the diving moral scales and found the king 'too light'.

CHAPTER 5

v.28 *Peres* means 'divided'. God was shattering the Empire and giving it to the Medes and Persians. *(Upharsin* and *peres* both are the same word.)

v.29 The Robing

In a futile attempt to escape the judgment of God, the king clothes Daniel in purple and proclaims him *the third ruler in the kingdom.*

4. Belshazzar's Fall

v.30 *In that night....* There is a last night for every nation and there is a last night for every man, woman, boy, and girl. . .
>*Prepare to meet thy God.* Amos 4:12

[History relates that Cyrus, the King of Persia, diverted the water of the Euphrates River (it flowed through the middle of Babylon) around the city, during that extended drunken feast of Belshazzar, and marched his army by the dry land of the river inside the city, while the king and his crowd were carousing at the annual feast of the gods.]

v.31 This verse discloses that *Darius the Median* seized the kingdom at about the age of 62 years. *See Dan.9:1.* Though Cyrus led the army assault that conquered Babylon, it was done in the name of Darius. Daniel 6:28 shows that Daniel was aware that Cyrus had led in the capture of the city Babylon but the Medes were the leading power in her destruction. *Isa.13:17*

Chapter 6

Following their incredible military upset, the Medes and Persians are now in control.

1. Daniel's Conduct

v.1 Darius was now ruler over Babylon. Prophecy had been fulfilled. The Babylonian head of gold had been replaced by the silver arms and breast of the Meads and Persians. *Dan.2:31, 32, 39*

v.2 Daniel was selected to be prime minister; he was no longer a young man at this time – nearly 90 years old.
God can use us regardless of our age. Some of the most prominent people in history have been elderly:

- William Gladstone was Prime Minister of Great Britain at age 83.
- Michelangelo did his immortal painting 'The Last Judgment' at age 89.
- John Wesley, founder of Methodism was still preaching many times a day at age 88.
- Thomas Edison was still inventing at age 90.
- J.C. Penney was still in business at age 95.
- Ronald Regan at age 77 was still President of the United States.
- Caleb was 85 years old when he said '***give me this mountain***' *Josh.14:12*. He asked for a tough assignment – one with mountains, giant and wall cities. He wanted a great blessing and knew such blessings do not come through easy assignments.

CHAPTER 6

- At the time of this writing I am in the sunset years of my life. While my body is old my fellowship with the Lord is more precious each day. God says *For which cause we faint not; but though our outward man perish, yet the inward man is renewed day by day.* 2 Cor. 4:16 And the Psalmist said *O God, thou hast taught me from my youth: and hitherto have I declared thy wondrous works. Now also when I am old and greyheaded, O God, forsake me not; until I have shewed thy strength unto this generation, and thy power to every one that is to come.* Ps.71:17-18

As we grow old we have the presence that God is with us. *My presence shall go with thee, and I will give thee rest.* Ex.33:14 Just because we are elderly don't write us off, or put us out to pasture. In God's service there is no 'retiring".

> The Secret Place
> In the secret of His presence
> How my soul delights to hide:
> O, How precious are the lessons
> Which I learned at Jesus' side!
> Earthly cares can never vex me
> Neither trials lay me low;
> For when Satan comes to tempt me
> The secret Place I go.

2. Daniel's Character

Daniel's prosperity and success made him the object of jealousy. Why? He was where the princes wanted to be. Envy exists in the best and worst of all communities and churches. 'Break him at any cost!' Superior goodness and godliness in others cause envy in the weaker souls. Prayer would help.

v.3 the *Excellent Spirit* in Daniel

The word **excellent** means
- to abound
- to be over, and above
- to be beyond measure
- to exceed bounds
- to be preeminent
- to excel

This was Daniel's rugged native ability that God had endowed him with. This turned the other two presidents and the 120 princes *v.1* green with envy.

Daniel was Faultless (not corrupt)

No error or fault was found in him. He did not make error or unwise decisions in the matters of the kingdom. There was no shadiness or dishonesty in any detain in civil matter.

v.4 Daniel was Faithful

Daniel was reliable, dependable, and trustworthy.

v.5 Daniel's God

The 120 princes and the two Gentile presidents agree that Daniel was clean in his character and conduct of business affairs. They arrived at a corporate conclusion that the only way they might entrap him might be concerning the Law of his God, The Almighty God who had sent judgment on the kings of Babylon, both Nebuchadnezzar and Belshazzar before them. Thus they moved to elevate themselves through a scheme to destroy Daniel. *See Acts 24:13-21; 1 Pet.4:12-16*

3. Daniel's Conspirators

v.6   The Plot
Envy seeks to get ahead by discrediting others. The two presidents and the 120 princes were out to get rid of Daniel at any cost. They entered into a colluded agreement that they would rush emotionally upon the king, with feigned love for him, and cry out, **King Darius, live for ever** - though they cared not if he died that day. They were out 'for the kill', to secure a means of publicly getting rid of Daniel.

vs.7-8   The Plan
1. It Deified God
Thou shalt have no other gods before me. *Ex.20:3* All prayers were to be directed to the king thereby honouring him as a god. This sent him on an ego trip.
2. It Deceived the King
They made it appear that their suggestion was unanimously agreed by all in high office. This was a lie; Daniel was not even consulted. They pulled the wool over the eyes of Darius.
3. It Dared
When the law was made it could not be altered. They knew Daniel prayed three times a day to the God of Heaven. Now they dare him to pray.

v.9 *King Darius signed the....decree*

The decree was 30 days and No Prayer. If that kind of law was passed in the U.S.A. - I am afraid it would not bother a great many at all.

4. Daniel's Courage

v.10 Daniel an example of prayer.
He was:
- **Fearless** *v.10* – He knew that the writing was signed; that no one was to make any petition to any god or man for 30 days. *He went into his house* to pray. He was not afraid.
- **Faithful** *v.4* – Daniel was devoted to God and duty.
- **Faultless** *v.4* – Daniel was not corrupt in business affairs.
- **Firm** *v.5* – Daniel's enemies found no occasion against him except concerning the law of his God. He stood firm.
  - **Had a Place to Pray** *v.10* – His house, his chamber
  - **He prayed *toward* Jerusalem** *v.10* His home land: Jerusalem, the place of worship. *2 Chr.6:36-39*
  - **He had posture in Prayer** *v.10* – Kneeling. [This is the most proper gesture in prayer. It is most expressive of humility, reverence and submission to God and His will.]
  - **He had a Period of Prayer** *v.10* – ***three times a day***. They passed a law against praying but they couldn't **keep** him from praying.
  - **He had a purpose in Prayer** *v.10* – Giving Thanks.

CHAPTER 6

One of the growing sins of our day is the sin of ingratitude. This is one of the signs of the end of this age (Church-age) preceding the rapture of the Church. *2 Tim.3:2*

5. Daniel's Crisis

v.11 The Assemble Enemies
The spies watched Daniel's window; his faith was put to the severest test. *2 Pet.4:12-16* Notice that the attacked came when Daniel was praying. More than likely you're not going to get attached when you're on the golf course or the tennis courts. The real attacks of the enemy will come when you're in prayer.

v.12 The Answer of the King
These 'Peeping Toms' went directly to the king and asked him whether or not he had **signed a decree** and stature according to the law of the Medes and Persians; that any found praying to or toward any god other than him, for 30 days would be put to death. Publicly he affirmed that this was true, not knowing what they had done; that they had sought to deceive him, and entrap Daniel to put him to death.

v.13 The Accusers
They were careful to point out that Daniel was a conquered foreigner. According to oriental custom punishment must be executed on the evening in which the accusation was made. This was the surety of getting rid of Daniel, but they failed to take into account Daniel's God!

v.14 The Angry King

He was angry with himself for signing the decree - he *was sore displeased.* Darius realized he had been duped by the two presidents and the 120 princes. His pride had been his downfall. He spent all day trying to undo his immutable law. Darius did not want to see Daniel killed. So he tried to find means to escape the force of the unchangeable law, to no avail.

v.15 The law had to be enforced. Daniel enemies sensed that delay would not be helpful to their evil intend, they press upon the king to execute the law.
Religious persecution has usually wrought its iniquities in the name of the law.

The Able Deliverer

v.16 The Silences of Daniel

Knowing the kind of person Daniel was - one can believe that he faced the challenge courageously. He was marched to the den, which was perhaps some distance from his home. The king was probably already there. A knowing look may have passed between the two as Daniel arrived. Daniel silently inquiring regarding the thinking of the king, and the king trying to reassure him that he was opposed to what was happening. Daniel served God continually.

Can it be said of you my Christian friend, that you serve God 'continually'; all the time. How often we sin against our Lord by the harsh words, by unkindness, by overreacting before we know all the details, or by neglected duty. May God help us to be such a witness to His Grace.

v.17 The Seal; The Signet
And a stone was brought, and laid upon the mouth of the den. Adam Clark writes "The same precaution was taken by the Jews, in the case of the burial of our blessed Lord; and this very thing has served as one of the strongest proofs of the certainty of His resurrection, and their unmixed wickedness."

The stone was sealed first by the king to assure that the lords would not go beyond what the degree demanded in order to guarantee Daniel's death. Then the lords sealed the stone to prevent the king from interfering to rescue Daniel. God works behind the seals and locks of men.

6. Daniel's Compensation

v.18 The Miserable Night
The king took no food, heard no music, and enjoyed no sleep. The king knew that he had been party to a serious injustice, and it lay heavily on his conscience. He did not wish to lose a valuable officer as Daniel; and felt guilty in the part he had unknowingly played in putting Daniel where he was. He probably also was ashamed at having been so easily tricked through flattery.

The Morning Discovery

<u>v.19</u> *Then the king arose very early in the morning, and went in haste unto the den of lions.*

Three kings were there!
  1. The King of Beasts – the Lion

Be sober, be vigilant; because your adversary the devil, as a roaring lion, walketh about, seeking whom he may devour. 1 Peter 5:8

2. The King of Medo-Persia; Darius
Somehow Darius hoped that the God of Daniel would come and deliver him. Darius could not deliver Daniel because of the unchangeable Medo-Persian law. *v.8*

3. The King of Kings was there
The Incarnate Son of the Living God was there to deliver Daniel.

v.20 Hope against hope, Darius cries out to Daniel in the Lion's Den.
The Question:
Was God able to save you?

v.21 **The Answer**:
O king, live for ever. There is no hint of reproach on Daniel's part against the king for his foolishness that had brought him so near death.

v.22 *My God hath sent his angel, and hath shut the lions' mouths.*

v.23   The Mighty God of Daniel
No manner of hurt was found upon him, because he believed in his God. You may get into a lions den but in God's good time He will bring you out.

v.24   The Merciless Execution
It may be questioned as to why the accuser's wives and children suffered the same fate. First of all, Darius was a

Gentile king. Persian law and custom was such that when the leader of the household was guilty, then the household must have been party to it and so were dealt the same fate. Darius would not know Hebrew law or the laws of God concerning judgment on the guilty. Hebrew law, the Law of God, very clearly protected fathers and sons and families from the same fate. The children would not suffer for the iniquity of the fathers nor the fathers for the iniquity of the children. *(Read carefully Ezek.18:1-4, 19-24)*
In the case of Achan, he and his whole family must have been party to his hiding the accused articles in the family tent. In this case the whole family was judged by the Lord. *Josh.7* Otherwise God would have been violating His own Word.

It is the same here with the accusers of Daniel. The accusers would undoubtedly tell their families about the decree. No one was to petition any god for 30 days. When Daniel was caught, the accusers would tell their families. If this was so, then the Lion's den was just judgment for their false accusations against the old man, the Prophet of God, Daniel.
There is, on the other hand, a Law of God, the law of retribution after its kind. *Read carefully Prov.26:27; 28:10; Ps.7:15-16; 9:15-16; Eccles.10:8-9; Prov.19:5; Luke 6:38.* Haman is another example. *Esther 7:9-10*

The Magnificent Dominion

1. Man's Dominion

The Earth
Gen.1:26. The first man is on the earth. Earthly; 1 Cor.15:49 If you want to bear the image of the Heavenly 1 Cor.15:49 you must confess your guilt as a sinner:

repent, turn from and forsake your sin and ask God to save you for Jesus sake. For whosoever shall call upon the name of the Lord shall be saved. Rom.10:13

v.25   The Kings Decree to all the earth.
Darius writes to all people, nations, and languages that dwell on the earth. Just as in Daniel 3:39 the King of Babylon had done. Then King Darius said Peace be multiplied unto you.

v. 26 The Decree

That in every dominion of my kingdom men tremble and fear before the God of Daniel

> The Reason for the Decree
> - He is the Living God
> - He is the Steadfast God
> - His Kingdom shall never be destroyed
> - His Dominion is Forever
> - He Delivers and Rescues
> - He works Signs and Wonders in Heaven and the Earth
> - He Delivered Daniel from the power of the Lions.

2. God's Dominion
v.27
- *Heaven*
- *Earth*
- He *inhabiteth eternity* Isa.57:15
- *His dominion is an everlasting dominion, which shall not pass away:* Dan.7:14

CHAPTER 6

- *.... The kingdoms of this world are become the kingdoms of our Lord, and of his Christ; and he shall reign for ever and ever.* Rev.11:15

v.28　The Prosperity of Daniel

The reason **Daniel prospered** is because God was with him. Daniel was protected by the power of God. So we have seen:

- Daniel in his public life – Purity
- Daniel in his private life – Prayer
- Daniel in his personal life – Patience.

Chapter 7

The Four Great Beasts

1. The Introduction of the vision

v.1   When Daniel Dreamed
In the first year of Belshazzar king of Babylon.
Chapters 7 and 8 actually take place between chapters 4 and 5. In chapter 4, Nebuchadnezzar was humbled for seven years before he was restored. In chapter 5, the kingdom was taken from Nebuchadnezzar's grandson, Belshazzar. Here, however, Belshazzar had just come into power and it was at this time Daniel had another vision...

What Daniel Dreamed

v.2   Striving Winds
- **Their Identity** - The *four winds* are reference to the unseen satanic forces at work in the world. Satan is **the prince of the power of the air**, *Eph.2:2* He has at his command an invisible army.
- **Their Plurality** - They are four in number. That is, they are global and universal in their scope.
- **Their Activity** - They stir the nations. They cause unrest, upheaval, and tumult. ***The sea*** in Revelation 17:15 is a symbol of the nations and is a reference to the Gentile nations that are hostile to God and Israel.

CHAPTER 7

v.3 The Stormy Waves

The four beasts coming up out of the sea, **diverse one from another**, represent four world empires. Isa.57:20 tells us that the nations - in their confusion, sorrow, distress and perplexity - **are like the troubled sea,** and this a fitting scene from which great empires arise. Verse 17 explains that these four beasts exist as four kings; so that in this matter no ground is left for speculation. These four beasts represent the beast-like character in growling, greedy, unregenerate men; in anarchy against God, as they appear in Rev.13:1-18.

2. The Information in the Vision

1. The First Beast: a Lion; The Babylonian Empire (Reign 66 to 70 yrs.)

The seed of Babylon was planted in Genesis 10:8-10 and 11:1-9. Nebuchadnezzar was the genius and the real builder of the Babylonian Empire which existed approximately 66 to 70 years. He ruled 45 of those years.

v.4 The Ravenous Lion

A lion with **eagle's wings** and **a man's heart**; This was an emblem of authority, strength, and speed. That lion was Nebuchadnezzar who swooped down like a spread-winged eagle upon its prey, with pride and self glory, until his wings were plucked by mental derangement or recessive nature, and until he acknowledged God. Then he was lifted upon his feet, upright from his beast-like, grass-eating posture, as a man dependent upon God. Dan.4:34-37 Babylon is often referred to as a lion Jer.4:7 and an Eagle. Jer.49:22.

2. The Second Beast: a Bear; The Medo-Persia Empire (Reign 207 yrs.)

v.5 The Rapacious (to take by force) Bear

A bear is slow, awkward, and lumbering, depending on brute force to conquer; certainly a picture of Persia. Persia often won battles by brute force and sheer strength. Xerxes expedition against Greece was done with 2,000,000 men. **One side** of the bear is raised, meaning the Persians - who took the upper hand of the Medes in their historic union.

The *three ribs* are the three kingdoms conquered by Persia: History has revealed that the territories were:
- Lydia – in 546
- Babylon – in 539
- Egypt – in 525

These three nations formed a triple alliance to check the powers of Persia, but they were destroyed.
The bear was:
- Ponderous
- Powerful
- Persistent

The armies of the Medo-Persian Empire did indeed *devour much flesh* as they marched across the battlefields.

3. The Third Beast – The Grecian Empire
(Reign just over 300 years)

(This empire was led by Alexander the Great)

v.6 The Rapid Leopard

The Grecian Empire (just over 300 years and into the century preceding the birth of Christ.); **the empire that astonish the world** by it's exceptional swiftness in conquering the world and symbolized by **the Leopard, even swifter with** *four wings.* In 8 years time the Greeks marched and conquered more than 11,000 miles of territory from Greece to India. Alexander died on June 13, 323 B.C. Its four heads point to the division of the Grecian Empire into four parts after Alexander's death. Dan.8:21-22 Each of the four segments was under the command of a General as follows:

Egypt and Palestine ruled by **Ptolemy**
North Syria ruled by **Seleucus**
Acedonia and Thrace ruled by **Cassander**
Asia Minor ruled by **Lysimachus**

4. The Fourth Beast – The Roman Empire

The Roman Empire gradual growth was in the 3rd century BC and its gradual decline was in the 3rd century AD. Its zenith was AD 117.

v.7 The Raging Beast

This wild beast defiles comparison. It was a hybrid (*diverse from all the beast that were before it*) and thus had no known beast by which to compare it.
Here are eight characteristics of the beast:

1. ***Dreadful*** - Dreaded by all nations. Not only was pagan Rome dreaded, and the name of Rome filled the world with terror for 700 years; but since the fall of pagan Rome, Papal (religious) Rome has filled the world with terror.

2. **Terrible** – bringing a reign of terror to all people of the earth.
3. **Strong** – exceeding strong Dan.2:40
4. **Great Iron Teeth** – crushing
5. **Devoured** – destruction
6. **And brake in pieces** – It reduced Macedonia to a Roman Province about one hundred and sixty-eight years before Christ; all those kingdoms, Pergamos, Syria, and Egypt, all Roman rule from a hundred to sixty years before Christ. And it subdued many other provinces and kingdoms. So that it could indeed be said to **devour the whole earth** v.23 and **tread it down, and break in pieces** everywhere its legions were carried. Therefore, in a very real sense it became the empire of the whole world. .... **that there went out a decree from Caesar Augustus, that all the world should be taxed** Luke 2:1. Rome actually ruled or potentially ruled all the world. That is to say, for instance, they ruled China; they ruled the far-off tribes not under the Roman legions. Here's how they did it. Rome was the supreme arbiter of all the differences among the nations of the world. It was the final court – just like the United Nations that was established to preserve peace among the nations which they will never succeed in doing. And so Rome, either actually or potentially, ruled the world. Here are two nations far apart who would get into war. So they would come to Rome and Caesar to arbitrate, and for his trouble of arbitration he said "you pay me so much tax." So all the world sent tribute to Rome. Therefore taxation is the test of rule or power.
7. **Diverse - from all the beast that were before it**, because it had no name. Whatever cruelty might have been attached to the lion and leopard and

bear – all of it should be summed up and attached to this one beast – the nameless beast.
8. ***and it had ten horns.*** – Horns means power everywhere you find it.

5. The Restoration of the Roman Empire

v.7   The Ten Horns
The fourth beast is symbol of the old Roman Empire; the fourth of four kingdoms in succession. The ten horns symbolize ten kingdoms in the latter days; the last form of the old Roman Empire. *vs. 7-8; 23-24; Rev. 13: 17:8-17*

v.8   The Tiny Horn
- **Its coming** – *came up among* the 10 horns. The little horn came up last after the ten horns were full grown.
- **Its conquests** – It ***plucked up*** three of the 10 horns ***by the roots***, symbolizing the Antichrist, coming in the days of the formation of Rome into ten kingdoms. He will overthrow three of them and the others will submit to him without further war. *vs. 8-24; Rev. 17:11-17*
- **Its Character** – ***Eyes like the eyes of a man*** – intelligence - ***and a mouth speaking great things***. This little horn is a man, the Antichrist, who speaks blasphemies against God.   *vs. 8-25;   Dan. 11:36; Rev. 13:1-5; 17:3*

6. The Return of Jesus Christ

v.9   The Ancient of Days
Daniel saw the thrones of kings ***cast down***. The ***Ancient of days*** sat on His throne. The above language unmistakably refers to the throne of God who is the

Ancient of days – The Eternal. Fire is ever the symbol of the Holiness of God and His Righteousness, which is judgment against sin. *2 Thes.1:8; Heb.12:29.*

v.10 The whole scene points to the Great White Throne Judgment, when the books will be opened and all the unsaved will be judged out of those books; Revelation 20:11-14 clearly confirms this. The scene here then actually brings us in time to Eternal Judgments of God seen in Revelation by John. It harmonizes with what Daniel is seeing here.

v.11   The Awful Retribution on the Little Horn

Because of the diabolical ways (of the Devil) and the blasphemous boasting of the little horn, the judgment that is pronounced against him in Heaven will be executed on earth. The destruction of the beast's body can only mean the empire he represents will be destroyed. The burning of his body is in keeping with the doctrine of God's final retribution from which there is no escape.

v.12   As for the Rest of Beasts

The difference between the first three beasts and the fourth beast is clearly brought out in this verse. The first three ceased to rule as kingdoms because their power was taken from them.
1. The Babylonian Empire was absorbed by the Medo-Persian Empire
2. The Medo-Persian Empire was absorbed by the Grecian Empire
3. The Grecian Empire was absorbed by the Roman Empire.

The Babylonian, Medo-Persian, and Grecian Empires continued into their successor's empire, but not with dominion. The revived Roman Empire will incorporate the features of all the former empires. *Rev.13:2.* Perhaps that is what is meant by the former empires having *their lives prolonged* 'for a time'.

7. The Reign of the Redeemer

v. 13 The identity of the *Son of man* is our Lord Jesus Christ. He is returning with clouds of deity with power and great glory. *Matt.24:30* As He draws near to the Ancient of days He is ushered into His presence. He is going there for one purpose to be achieved; it is so that He might receive the title deed of Planet Earth and become the rightful heir of all things.

v.14 This is the moment when the Father 'will give to His Son His inheritance of the nations of the world'. This is the fulfillment of Psalms 2:6-9. The Lord Jesus Christ will have dominion over *all people, nations, and languages* for His entire one thousand year millennial reign *Rev.20:4-6*. After the Millennium, the Lord's reign over all saints will continue for all eternity in the *new heavens and a new earth. 2 Pet.3:10-13.*

3. The Interpretation of the Vision

1. Daniels Puzzled Request
v.15   His Grief
The effect of the vision was that *Daniel was grieved*. He was troubled in his spirit, mind and it affected him physically. Spirit, soul, and body were affected by the sight of the vision.

v.16   His Guidance
Daniel confessed his human ability to grasp the meaning of the vision. He turned to one of the celestial beings (probably an angel) standing before the throne and sought

enlightenment and willingly the angelic attendant explained the meaning of the vision. Daniel made known his desire to obtain certainty of the truth of the vision. That is what God's children always ought to do when they are in uncertainty about some part of Scripture. They must not want to remain uncertain but allow themselves neither rest nor peace of mind until they have obtained the necessary light.

2. Daniel's Prophetic Review

1. The Five Kingdoms

v.17 The Four Passing Kingdoms - The four beasts represented Babylon, Medo-Persia, Greece and Rome.

v.18 The Fifth Kingdom - After the four kingdoms run their course, another kingdom, possessed by the *saints of the most High* will prevail. The kingdom will begin with the Millennial kingdom and endure *for ever, even for ever and ever*.

2. The Fourth Kingdom

The dominating rule of the fourth beast *vs.19-20* **then I would know the truth of the fourth Beast** *v.19*. Daniel had a desire to know the truth about the fourth beast. We need to put more emphasis on learning spiritual matters than secular matters. We need to learn more about eternal things than temporal things.

v.19 *His Nails of Brass* - An additional feature to all others listed in verse 7, the claws were dreadful and terrible. John Calvin says it was "endued with such savage madness as not only to attack all things by it

CHAPTER 7

unusual violence, but to tear, lacerate and devour all things." Such indeed was the ruthless brutality cruel destructiveness of Rome.

v.20 The Eleventh horn that came up among the ten horns - It is to be understood that this little horn (what he is called v.8) is yet to rise out of Gentile governments in disarray signified by the number 10. The 'Little Horn", eleventh horn, the cruel ruler is to be the Antichrist, more cruel that Antiochus Epiphanes. *Dan.8:9; 12-25. 2 Thes.2:4-10; Rev.19:20.*
A mouth that spake very great things; That is against God Himself. - - *whose look was more stout than his fellows.* He is described as '*stout*'; a common Hebrew word in the O.T. translated as 'stout' once, 'many' 190 times and 'great' 128 times. In verse 20 it means 'great' - thus the word described the pre-eminence of the beast over his fellows (i.e. the other 10 horns: kings) and hence seems to be a copy of the pre-eminence of the Lord Himself.

v.21 In Revelation 6:1 the Antichrist comes riding on a white horse imitating Christ by way of contrast with the rider (Christ) of Revelation 19:11; the Antichrist being a deceiver *2 Thes.2:9-10* **made war with the saints and prevailed against them.** The Antichrist will persecute the tribulation saints throughout the last three and one half years of the tribulation until Christ comes back to conclude the Battle of Armageddon and set up His Millennial kingdom. *Rev.12:13-17; 19:11-21*

v.22 The Over Ruling of Heaven - The 'little horn' was winning the victory until the **Ancient of day came** (second coming of Jesus) and stopped the attack upon His saints. Now the tables are turned, and those who were persecuted are placed in the position of judges over the wicked horn. Their position includes the right to rule as well. *Rev.20:4*

vs.23-24 **The Fourth Kingdom and it king** - The angel indicated that the Roman Empire would pass through three stages of History.

- **The first stage** could be called 'the Beast of conquering' stage *v.23*. Rome would devour and crush a much greater area than the earlier three kingdoms would. The first stage was descriptive of the ancient Roman Empire.

- **The second stage** could be called 'the ten horn or ten kingdom' stage. *v.24* The angel declared that eventually the ten kings would rise out of the fourth kingdom. Since the ten horns were part of the fourth beast *v.7* this meant that eventually the Roman Empire would have ten rulers or would consist of a ten nation confederation. As noted in chapter 2, since the ancient Roman Empire never consisted of a ten nation confederation, this form of the fourth kingdom must be future. Sometime in the future the Roman Empire will be revived in the form of a ten nation confederation.

- **The third stage** of Rome's history could be called 'the little horn or antichrist' stage. *v.24*
  The little horn, who is actually an eleventh king, will arise. He is different in person and in time – since he arises later than the ten. He will come to power by subduing three of the ten kings, which will give him the balance of power.
  From the description given of the king it is obvious that he will be the 'ultimate man', the greatest expression of the man – centered manic, which has

CHAPTER 7

been driving man to reject God's rule since the fall of man in Eden. *2 Thes.2:3-4; 7-8* He will be the one whom John called the Antichrist. *1 John 2:18*

v.25 The Activity of the Dictator - To utter **great words against the most High**. This had been the activity of the religious when the Lord was here. **And he open his mouth in blasphemy against God ......and his tabernacle and them that dwell in heaven.** *Rev.13:6; 16:11* The reference to both God and **his Tabernacle** allows us to interpret **the most High** as either the Most High God, or the Heavenly Places.

He will **wear out the saints**. This will be Satan's last attempt to destroy the Jewish race during the great tribulation.

He will **change times and laws**. He will attempt to change moral and natural laws of the Universe, apparently without success. *v.25* An example of this may be seen in the attempt made by the leaders of the French Revolution to replace the seven day week established by God with a ten day week. Their efforts failed. On the other hand, the Antichrist, energized by Satan, will be able to perform miracles which will cause many to accept his blasphemous claims and become his ardent followers. *2 Thes.2:8-11* The duration of this change will be the period known as **a time** (one year) **and times** (two years) **dividing of time** (one half year) which will be three and one half years or **forty and two months**. *Rev.13:5*

v.26 The little horns career will come to a sudden and disastrous end. *also v.11* The process of judgment takes place throughout the last seven years of the tribulation until the final judgment in Revelation 19:1-21. The court of Heaven will sit; the **Ancient of days** will pronounce judgment; and the **Son of man** will execute the sentence. **They shall take away his dominion** marks the end of the Gentile rule.

3. The Fifth Kingdom

v.27 The kingdom from above (the Millennial Reign of Christ *Rev.20:4*) will be set up and **the saints of the most High** receive the kingdom; and the kingdoms of this earth will become the Kingdoms of God and His Christ. *Rev.11:15* Satan had his throne on the earth and gave it to the beast, the 'little horn'. The 'little horn' then will be dethroned and the true King of Kings enthroned upon the Holy Hill of Zion. God will share this kingdom with His people and they shall reign with Him. *Rev.5:10; 11:15; 20:4*

3. Daniel's Personal Reaction

v.28 This is the completion of the vision. Daniel's thoughts (***cogitations***) trouble him. It affected his countenance, but he **kept the matter** in his heart before the Lord. In due time, he wrote it down under inspiration of the Holy Spirit as we have it in Daniel 7. It can be assumed that, while Daniel did not understand fully all the details of the vision, as often times the Prophets experienced, *1 Pet.1:11-12* he did see the correspondence between the 'metallic world-kingdom' of the image-dream *Dan.2:1-49* and the 'beast kingdoms' vision he had received. It was the additional revelation given to Daniel that caused his concern.

The additional portions of the fourth beast kingdom - The ten horns and the rise and activities of the little horn. These parts were additional truth given to Daniel, which were not given to Nebuchadnezzar.

CHAPTER 7

He was surprised at his vision and could not understand it all. Soon the Lord gave him more to think about, and more details of what will happen in the end.

This is the end of the chapters where Daniel used the Aramaic language, beginning in chapter 2:4. For the rest of the book, Daniel wrote in the Hebrew language, as the Holy Spirit used in most of the Old Testament.

Chapter 8

The Persian Ram and the Greek Goat

1. Mark the time and Place

The first two verses of this chapter are to be regarded as introductory

v.1   The Time
In the third year of the reign of King Belshazzar. The events of chapter 7 occurred during the first year of the reign of Belshazzar. *7:1* The visions described in this chapter were seen two years later, but before chapter 9.

v.2   The Place
The place of the vision was *in the palace* in *Shushan... in the province of Elam* (Persia) as he was *by the river Ulai.* See *Esther 1:1-4* Shushan was the winter capital of the Persian Empire. It is interesting that Daniel and Ezekiel (captive Prophets in Babylon) each had their visions by a river. *Ezek.1:1-4; 3:15-23*

2. The Three Personages of the Vision and the Little Horn

The First Personage

The Ram symbol of Persia
v. 3   The Horns: Medo-Persia alliance
One horn *was higher that the other, and the higher came up last.* The balance of power with the coming of Cyrus tipped from the Medes, permanently to Persia. It remained that way for the foreseeable future. The

CHAPTER 8

dominant influence in their shaky partnership was attributable to the skilful maneuvering of Cyrus who achieved his position by his secret artfully sly action. In other words – he was a thief.

v.4   The Powerful Hold

The ram was pushing westward, and northward, and southward – extending its conquest in these directions. Persia lay eastward from Media, and the conquest of the empire was not extended eastward beyond Persia. The result was that this mighty empire spread from India to Ethiopia, which at that time was the known world.

- **The Power of the Ram was Irresistible.**
  No beast might stand before him, neither was there any that could deliver out of his hand – or in other words, the nations that attempted to resist the invader were not able to do so with success; and no nation was able to deliver a conquered country out of the hand of the conqueror. This condition continued, of course, only so long as it was ordained in the plan of God that the Medo-Persian Empire should endure.

- **The Ram** *did according to his will.*
  The empire was not dominated by any other power, and pursued its course according to the will of its rulers.

- **It** *became great.*
  The empire rose to such prominence - to such greatness among the empires of the earth - that it was without an equal. It became in the truest sense of the word, a world empire.

The Second Personage

v.5 This *he goat* was the acknowledged symbol of Greece.
The face of the whole earth – an indication of the massive scale of the conquest.
And touched not the ground - Alexander the Great with his army of 35,000 men moved with such speed that he is pictured as 'not even touching the ground'. He conquered the then 'known world' in less that ten years.

>Verse 21 tells us *the rough goat* symbolizes the Grecian Empire; the notable horn is Alexander the Great: Greece's first king.

v. 6 the fury of the goat against the ram.
and ran unto him in the fury of his power.

v.7 His *choler* (bitterness) against the ram:
....and he was moved with choler against him.
The goat *smote the ram ....cast him down to the ground, and stamped upon him*. Alexander's conquest against Persia was lightning fast.

v.8 **His death** - Having gone to the top he fell! At the summit of his well decorated career something mysterious happened. A brief obituary records the death of Alexander. One short sentence: *The great horn was broken*. He was great, he was strong, but now he is gone. After 12 years at the top of the world, how the mighty are fallen! He died tragically at the age of 33 in June 323 B.C. Sadly he conquered the world, but not himself.

CHAPTER 8

The Four Horns - Four of Alexander's generals divided up the empire, each one controlling certain countries. This fits in the prophecy of Daniel which the Lord gave him 200 years before these things came to pass.

The Third Personage

The Coming of the Little Horn
The 'little horn' is Antiochus Epiphanes who came out of Syria, one of the **four notable** *v.8* kingdoms into which Alexander's empire was divided. He ruled Syria from 175 - 164 B.C.

v.9 The little horn expands his borders.
The **little horn...waxed exceeding great**, **towards the south,** (Egypt) **toward the east,** (Armenia) **and toward the pleasant land** (Israel). This is called the **pleasant land**, *Jer.3:19* and a **glorious land**. *Dan.11:16,41* He is not the same **little horn** as the one in chapter 7; that **little horn** came out of the ten-nation confederation, which is the Antichrist. This **little horn** of chapter 8 comes out of the Seleucid family which ruled Syria, and is a picture, a foreshadowing, of the Antichrist that will come in the end time. *Rev.13* The **little horn** of chapter 8 has already come.

v.10 The conquests of the Little Horn
He had an inbred hatred towards the Jewish people. He murdered thousands of them. He was anti-Semitic. In Scriptures, the Jews, particularly the righteous Jews, are sometimes symbolized by **stars**. *Gen.15:5; 22:17; Dan.12:3; Rev.12:1*

It would appear that Satan empowered and energized him to such a degree that his policy of annihilation of the Jews would be a tool of Satan to prevent the birth of Jesus. Thankfully, his plan was not successful.

vs.11-12   **The Corruption of the Little Horn**
He profaned the Temple in the city of Jerusalem and carried out a purge of every form of worship associated with Judaism. He looted the Temple of its priceless treasures. He had the arrogance to remove the golden altar of incense, the table of showbread and lampstand. After he successfully plunder and defiled the Temple he had it rededicated as a place of worship for Aeus who was the chief Greek god. He had a pagan altar built over the altar of God and commanded that regular sacrifices be replaced by the sacrifice of pigs. This was a curse to the Jews and an act of sacrilege towards God. The Jews labeled him 'Antiochus Epiphanes: the madman'! And so he was. This is what the Antichrist will do in the tribulation time. *2 Thes.2:4*

The time period permitted

v.13 Because of the Jews transgression God allowed Antiochus Epiphanes to persecute them and take away the daily sacrifice; but in this verse we read of a ***certain saint*** which asked ***how long*** this was to be allowed. ***Saint*** means 'holy one' and refers to an angel of God.

v.14 He prophesies that the sanctuary should be cleansed in 2300 days; or 6 years, 4 months and 20 days. Antiochus Epiphanes attached the sanctuary in the year 171 B.C. and in 165 B.C. The deprivation and corruption of this man ceased and the sanctuary was cleansed. This wicked man attacked the priests and the Scriptures. *v.12* Here, Israel, under Judas Maccabees, arose as a man, and cast this inhuman monster out to die (two years later) a miserable death.

Men may deny the Word of God but it stands infallible and unbroken and what it says will surely come to pass, exactly as God says.

3. The Troubled Prophet

The vision interpreted
This brings us to the ultimate application of the vision.

vs.15-16　These verses bring before us **Gabriel**, who is sent from heaven **to make** Daniel **understand the vision**.

v.17　Daniel was made **afraid** – a reverential fear of God;

v.18　He was brought low – fell on his face - making him unconscious of all around.　It was **a deep sleep**. [Preoccupation with Christ will make us forget all that goes on in this world.] He was made to stand - **He touched me, and set me upright**.
　...*having done all, to stand. Stand therefore...* Eph.6:13-14

4. The Terrible Power of the Persecutor

v.19　*The last end of the indignation.*
As we will see, some elements of the vision manifest the interpretive 'Law of double fulfillment'; that is, the vision describes a person (Antiochus Epiphanes) who lived and died several centuries after Daniel's lifetime and who foreshadows another individual (the Antichrist) yet to arrive on the scene.

Time appointed the end shall be. *also v.17*
The term likely has a dual meaning; referring to a time late in the period, defined by the empires described in these verses; and also the last day of human history and the time of the Antichrist.

v.20 *The ram* – the ***Media and Persia*** Empire

v.21 *The rough goat.* The Grecian Empire – ***the great horn that is between his eyes*** is Alexander the Great. He was the first great king who made Greece into an empire.

v.22 The ***broken*** horn and the ***four*** horns that ***stood up from it.*** *see v.8* Alexander died a young man at the age of 33, and his four generals divided up the empire, but none of them were as strong as Alexander.

The King of Fierce Countenance

The initial interpretation of these next three verses point to the man we have been just looking at, namely Antiochus Epiphanes. Prophecy, however, frequently has a double fulfillment. Partially this vision is fulfilled in Antiochus, but ultimately it will be fulfilled in the Antichrist.
- In the short term it is relevant to Antiochus.
- In the long term it is with regard to the Antichrist.

v.23 The Emergence of a Person

The spotlight is shining on a diabolical prince who will appear to the front of world events in the end times. He is a skilled politician and supremely competent in the art of double-dealing. He is enmeshed in a web of occultic influence and is a willing tool in the hand of the archenemy. He is a puppet and Satan is pulling the strings. He is the Antichrist.

v.24   The Enduement with a Power
He is a dark horse ridden by Satan. He holds the reins. The Devil is his paymaster. He is enabled and endowed with all mediums of darkness so that to the waiting world he is presented as the devil incarnate. Satan will be his mentor. All that he is and has come from the pit. He will perform a host of signs and wonders.

v.25   The Enactment of his Policy
His policy will be steamrolled through as he plays to the gallery in a valiant attempt to win their affection. And through his policy also **he shall cause craft to prosper in his hand;**

The expression of his pride. He will have an inflated ego and his successor will have given him a swollen head. And **he shall magnify himself in his heart**.

The explanation of the Phrase: *But he shall be broke without hand.* His fall is foretold. His doom is inevitable. He will be defeated by the Word of Christ at His re-entry to the world and will be **cast alive into the lake of fire**. *Rev.19:11-21*   There will be no human interference in his downfall – it is an act of God. No generation in history has had to face the problems our world now has to grapple with. World leaders are looking for someone with all the answers; so far that person has not been revealed *2 Thes.2:3-12* - but not for much longer.

Only time will show how accurate has been the prophecy of Daniel pertaining to the coming world leader.

The Effects of the Vision

v.26 *which was told is true* – a solemn affirmation that the vision was true.

wherefore shut thou up the vision - the sense seems to be 'but close up and keep safe' the vision!

For it shall be for many days - In the present day, we know that the vision was partially fulfilled in the time when Antiochus Epiphanes ruled, but we believe also that it will be completely fulfilled in the future in the Antichrist.

v.27 Daniel became *sick* about what he had seen and heard, but soon got better and went about *the king's business*. No true child of God neglects life's normal obligations and responsibilities. Indeed, his effective and efficient fulfillment of them is one of the most telling arguments for the reality and sincerity of his faith.

Chapter 9

1. The Prediction of Jeremiah
Jer.25:1-14; 29:10-14

The Promptings of Prayer

v.1 ***The first year of Darius*** was 539 B.C.; The year that Babylon fell to the Medes and the Persians. Daniel was cast into the lion's den under Darius the Mede. *Dan.6* The seventy weeks prophecy is now given to Daniel - under the reign of Darius the Mede.

v.2 ***Daniel understood*** from the Book of Jeremiah that the Babylonian captivity of the Jews was coming to a close. *Jer.25:11-12; 29:10*

2. The Prayer of Daniel

v.3 What did Daniel Do

He is interceding …He believed firmly the Word of God. He claimed the promise of God and began to pray. He threw open his window and drew near to God. He poured out his heart; he emptied his emotions.

The Penitence in Prayer
There were three useful aids to his season of prayer.
- His **fasting** – denying himself those things which were perfectly legitimate.
- He clothed himself in **sackcloth**; an act of self abasement
- He put **ashes** on his head; symbol of genuine humility and a sign of total grief.

The Particulars in the Prayer

v.4 As Daniel approached God he is overwhelmed with the sense of that he is just a man. He is stirred when he thinks of who God is
- A God of **Might**
- A God of **Majesty**
- A God of **Mercy**

vs.5-6   Here is a recognition of sin and also an identification of Daniel with his people as he consistently says '**we**'. He associated himself with them even though there is not blemish on his character.

There are five features enshrined in the confession of Daniel.
   1.   **We have sinned**; they missed the mark, they fell short of God's standard.
   2.   We **have committed iniquity**; they were crooked in their dealings and bent in their outlook.
   3.   We have **done wickedly**; they were lawless and ungodly.
   4.   We **have rebelled**; they revolted against God. They adopted a rebellious attitude and wanted to do their own thing.
   5.   **Even by departing from thy precepts**; They spurned His love and flatly rejected His Word. They were content to go in the opposite direction and depart further from Him.

vs.7-10 What a contrast between them and God

  1. **The Purity of God** - He is righteous *v.7*

CHAPTER 9

2. **The Purpose of God** - He Scattered them ...*all the countries whither thou hast driven them.* *v.7*
3. **The Pity of God** - To *our God belong mercies.* *v.9*
4. **The Pardon of God** - willing to Forgive. *v.9*
5. **The Promise of God** - He withheld His blessings. *v.10*

They have pushed His patience to the limits and even when he has been favorable towards them, they have retained the option to keep on sinning.

v.11 Moses warned Israel that they would bring the curse of God on themselves if they did not keep his law. *Deut.28:45-50; 29:19-21*

v.12 What God had foretold will ultimately come to pass, and so the Babylonian captivity 'confirmed' God's warning spoken centuries before. And it is the same for the future: God has **appointed a day, in the which he will judge the world in righteousness.** Acts 17:31 Men could not escape judgment in the Old Testament, and neither can men today - if they **neglect so great salvation.** Heb.2:3 The **judges** referred to are the leaders of the nation, so often being responsible for leading the nation down the sinful path.

v.13 The people should have known from the books of Moses that this trouble came from God; but they would not pray or repent of their sins or try to understand the truth. Sin blinds the minds of men, and prayer seems irrelevant and unnecessary.

v.14 From the time of Moses up to Nebuchadnezzar was about 900 years; during all this period **the Lord**

watched upon the evil. The word '***evil***' refers to the desolations of Jerusalem, as verse 12 and 13 show. God '***watched***' upon this in the sense that during the 900 years, He knew He would bring it to pass; likewise He watched the evil during the 70 years of captivity, knowing that it had to run its course until this period was completed. During the 900 years in which the people departed from the law, the necessity of judgment was ever before Him, causing Him to visit judgment upon the nation on many occasions. What mercy, what longsuffering God showed to His people. The same can be said of His people today. Israel had only themselves to blame. It was self-inflicted.

vs.15-19   The Petition in Prayer
A heartfelt plea; an impassioned request for God to 'step into the situation' is the burden on Daniel's heart.
- The city has been destroyed.
- The holy places have been desecrated.
- The Land has been left desolate.
- The people are the object of derision.

Daniel entreats God to intervene so that His name may be lifted up again. His honor is at stake. He cast himself upon God and throws himself upon the mercies of the God of Heaven.

vs.20-23   The Power in the Prayer
God interrupts Daniel while he was praying. The angel **Gabriel,** in the form of a man, came and touched Daniel, and he talked to him. He gave him the assurance that he would be able to understand the future of the nation Israel. His questions concerning her survival would be fully answered. God would draw back the curtain and give him a bird's-eye view of His plans for His earthly people.

CHAPTER 9

Daniel was *greatly* loved in Heaven. That was God's estimation of His servant. He was a man after His own heart. He matters to God. What a noble testimony!

3. The Prophecy of the Seventy Weeks

v.24 A Definition of the 70 years.
Among the Hebrews there were three classifications of weeks.

1. **Weeks of Days** – from one Sabbath to another. *Gen.2:2*
2. **Weeks of Years** – from one Sabbatical year to another Sabbatical year. *Gen.29:27*
3. **Weeks of seven times seven years** – or forty-nine (49) years. *Lev.25:8-13*

Here the Hebrew word 'seventy' is translated '*weeks*' as demanded by the context. But, the word means 'seventy sevens'. So we understand that the prophecy in these verses related to seventy (70) sevens (7) or four hundred ninety (490) years: A 70 weeks times 7 years equals 490 years. That '**years**', not days or months, are meant is evident for the fact that Daniel was thinking in terms of years as the angel Gabriel, came to speak to him. *v.2*

The Details of the 70 Weeks
The angel Gabriel first summarized what was to transpire in the seventy (70) weeks of years by listing six (6) important purposes of God's relating to the people; Israel; and the Holy city, Jerusalem.

1. ***To finish the Transgression*** – the word ***transgression*** means 'rebel'. It refers to the Jews

specific sin of rebellion against the rule of God. Deep rebellion brought deep affliction.

2. **To make an end of sins** – that is to put an end to daily sins of God's people. These will not end until the second coming of Jesus – when they (the Jews) will repent and find a fountain opened *for sin and for uncleanness*. Zech.13:1

3. **To make reconciliation for iniquity** – to provide atonement for sin. This is affected by the blood of Christ. There is coming a day of pardon for the Jewish people who will lament when they see the coming King. Zech.12:10-13 This takes place at the second coming of Christ.

4. **To bring in everlasting righteousness** – that is - to bring in a kingdom in which everlasting righteousness will prevail. It will be the Kingdom of God on earth. This is the thousand year reign of Christ on the earth; Rev.20:1-6. Israel will come into the good of the new covenant as outlined in Jeremiah 31:33-40.

5. **To seal up the vision and prophecy** - that is bring to completion by fulfillment all prophecies of Scripture. The word translated '*to seal up*' is the same word which was translated 'to make an end' in the phrase **to make an end of sins** earlier in this verse. It would appear that there is an intended relationship between the two phrases. The relationship is as follows: when Israel will make an end of its daily sins at the 490 years, then all revelation that came through vision and prophecy concerning God's chastening of Israel can be sealed up.

6. **To anoint the most Holy** – that is to anoint the religious service, the most Holy place, of as yet future, the millennial Temple. This will not be a Temple of type and shadows as in the Old

Testament, but one for service WITH the Lord present. *Ezek.43:4-5*

The Division of the 70 Weeks

v.25 We have seventy (70) weeks in verse 24. Gabriel explains that the seventy (70) weeks are divided into three (3) sections in verses 24 and 25.

1. *Seven weeks* of Years (49 years)
During this period of 49 years the city of **Jerusalem** was rebuilt; **the street....and the wall** were **built again**, ...**even in troublous times**. Under the leadership of Nehemiah, the walls of the city were repaired in fifty-two (52) days. *Neh.6:15* It apparently didn't take too much longer to clear out all of the debris and restore all the damage inflicted by Nebuchadnezzar. The seventy (70) weeks began with Nehemiah 2:1-8

2. Sixty-two (62) Weeks (434 years)
The second period sweeps on to Christ the **Messiah the Prince**. After the 49 years (or the 7 weeks) period, there was another period of 343 years (or 62 weeks) before the Messiah came as the Prince of Israel. The first cycle of the 49 years, while mentioned separately from the 434 years, is yet joined to it; therefore making to two cycles combined, totaling 483 years. This brings to the first coming of Christ - not however, to His birth, but apparently to the day He presented Himself to the nation of Israel as their Messiah Prince. In an official manner He did this only once - at the time of the triumphal entry into Jerusalem. *Matt.21:1-11* This event fulfilled the 69 weeks (or 483 years) of Daniel's 70 weeks (or 490 years).

Sir Robert Anderson in his book on *'Daniel the Coming Prince'* has calculated that from the first day Neh.2:1-8 to the last day when Jesus rode into Jerusalem; Matt.21:1-11 therefore a total of 173,880 days is based on the Hebrew calendar of 360 days per year. Remarkable that is equivalent to 483 years; just as the Prophet said it would be.

v.26   What will happen after the 69 weeks?

The question is answered in this verse. It should be noted that there is a gap now introduced between the 69th and 70th because of several very significant events predicted to come to pass after 62 weeks, following the first 7 weeks, making a total of 69 weeks or 483 years.

>   1. The *Messiah be cut off* – Christ crucified. *He came unto his own, and his own received him not.* John 1:11

>   *But not for himself* – the meaning evidently is that it was not for His own sins that He was cut off, but for the sins of others. Jesus knew no sin. *For he hath made him to be sin for us, who knew no sin; that we might be made the righteousness of God in him.* 2 Cor. 5:21

>   2.   The city and sanctuary will be destroyed - *and the end thereof shall be with a flood.* The flood refers back to the destruction of Jerusalem (70 A.D.). History records that Titus the Roman General, led four (4) Roman legions to besiege and destroy Jerusalem in 70 A.D.; also states that both the city and sanctuary would be destroyed by *the people of the prince that shall come.*" Interestingly enough *'the people'* or the Romans

CHAPTER 9

have already come, yet **the prince** or the Antichrist is still yet to come. The **prince** cannot refer to the Messiah Prince in verse 25 since the date of His coming was already carefully determined; rather this refers to a future prince or the Antichrist who was referred to in Daniel 7:8-9; 9:26

3. **War and desolation** will be the continuing experience of the people of Israel.
- The Gap period of time begins here.
- The gap period began when Christ made His triumphal entry into Jerusalem. *Matt.21:1-11*

I believe that the latter part of this verse **and unto the end of the war desolations are determined** is in the 'gap period'.

The interval is a period of unknown and it has lasted approximately 2000 years. This gap of time is the Church-age. There will be wars and desolations for the duration of the Church-age. This will be, and is currently, perilous times. *2 Tim.3:1-8* God is now calling a people out of the world to Himself, which makes up the body of Christ, or the Church. We do not know how much longer this period will last. The Church-age will end with the return of Christ to receive unto Himself His own. *1 Thes.4:16-17*

The Seventieth week (7 years)
Thus the 70th week, or the last 7 years of the 490 years involved in the prophecy, did not follow immediately after the end of the first 69 weeks, or 483 years. This indicates that the 7 years of Tribulation Period has not begun.

There is nothing unusual about this 'Gap' period of time found here in Daniel 9:26-27. Another example of such a 'gap' is found in Luke 4:18-19 where Jesus reads from Isaiah 61:2. ***To proclaim the acceptable year of the LORD,..*** He stops reading in the middle of the verse. This part of the verse was fulfilled in the Day of Jesus. This is Christ's first advent. Where the comma is indicates the 'gap' of time here in Isaiah 61:2, and the latter part of this verse is yet future ***and the day of vengeance of our God; to comfort all that mourn;*** This will be Christ's Second Advent. *1.Thes.1:7-10* The Church Age lies between the 69th and 70th week of Daniel.

The next event in God's program is the Rapture of the Church. The Church-age ends with Revelation Chapter 3; the Laodicea Church.

v.27 A Description of the 70th week

The Seven year Covenant
- The 70th week (7 years) begins after the Church has been caught up to heaven. *1.Thes.4:17*
- The Antichrist will make a covenant with the Jews the first 3 ½ years of the tribulation 'to protect them from their enemies'.

The Covenant Broken
In the midst of the 7 years the Antichrist will break the covenant with the Jews, causing the sacrifice (in the restored Temple) to cease and desecrate the Temple and will claim to be God and demand to be worshipped as God. *2 Thes.2:4* The abomination in this verse is the same that Jesus spoke of in Matthew 24:15.

'The ***abominations***' are 'detested things' connected with idolatry. Here, with the horrors of the Antichrist, ***Who opposeth and exalteth himself above all that is called God, or that is worshipped; so that he as God sitteth***

CHAPTER 9

in the temple of God, shewing himself that he is God.
2 Thes.2:4

The Antichrist will turn on the Jews, and they will flee into the mountains for refuge. Matt.24:16 The final period of 1 week (7 years) is dominated by the appearance of the Antichrist - who becomes the Jews protector and then their persecutor - until he is stopped by Christ on His return to earth. Rev.19:20

The seven year tribulation period runs from Revelation chapter 6 through chapter 19.

Chapter 10

1. Daniel's condition

The Revelation

v.1 *In the third year of Cyrus king* is 534 B.C., taking place about 4 years after the vision of the 70 weeks.
a thing was revealed unto Daniel…..the thing was true…..but the time appointed was long. This indicates that the final fulfillment was in the distant, not the immediate future.

He understood the thing, and had understanding of the vision. If God thus used the prophet as a vessel for the revelation of the future, He also gave him to understand what was revealed.

The Resolution

v.2 Daniel was so burdened for his people that he gave no thought to life's luxuries; He mourned and fasted *for 3 full weeks*.

v.3 This was rigorous time for Daniel, now a man past 90 years of age, yet he was following a lifetime practice. He was dedicated and determined. Dan.1:8

He is a man who is
- Instructed in the Purpose of God
- Interceding for the People of God
- Interested in the Work of God.

CHAPTER 10

2. A Crucial Question

Who was this Heavenly being?
v.4   Daniel was by the side of the River Hiddekel (ancient name of the Tigris River). The Tigris and Euphrates River are connected with the Garden of Eden. *Gen.2:14* Of old, God came down in the cool of the day to talk and walk with unfallen Adam; so He came down again to commune with His aged prophet Daniel.

1. The Terror

Who is this *certain man*?
vs.5-6   Here was no human being: the transcendent splendor of this one surpassed that of any angel or spirit being. A comparison of the description with those of Ezekiel 1:25-28 and Revelation 1:12-16 leaves no doubt that Daniel saw was the Son of the living God, Jesus Christ the Saviour of the world.

v.7   The men with Daniel didn't see the vision but they felt the terror of a powerful presence and hid themselves.

v.8   Daniel's companions abandoned him, forcing Daniel to stare at this *great vision* alone. If he was scared as they were, he couldn't do anything about it because his strength had failed him, leaving him to weak to run.

2. The Trance

v.9   Still he heard the great voice of the messenger. Daniel was so moved and disturbed that he fell with his face to the ground in a deep sleep. Daniel's humility in all this is a good example to us. He was not puffed up by reason of the abundance of revelations given him. He falls to the ground. Verse 8 leads to a physical effect, but verse 9 to a mental effect, as in a faint; or as it was, Daniel fell into a trancelike state, sapped of his strength.

3. The Communication of the Certain Man

v.10 The Touch
The touch of God awakened him and brought Daniel to his knees.

We need to be
- Touched by his power *Acts 1:8*
- Touched in Prayer *Jude:20*
- Touched in Pit *Matt. 18:33* – to show compassion
- Touched in Piety *1 Tim. 5:4*

To Respect; To Worship; To Reverence

v.11 The Trembling
Daniel was **greatly beloved** by God. God loves you, my friend, and if you are seeking to honor Him in your life as Daniel did, you are greatly beloved in Heaven.

God wanted Daniel to understand His Word.
In verses 11-21 the vision turns from the Lord (the Messiah) to a heavenly messenger who has been sent to Daniel. The messenger urged Daniel to make a special effort to understand what he was about to reveal. He told Daniel to stand up. He explained that the reason he had appeared was because he had been sent. It is not said who sent him; I believe it was Jesus whom Daniel had just seen in verses 5-6.

Daniel obeyed and stood on his feet, even though he was trembling. Yes, and we who may be called to witness some of the latter day scenes which pass before Daniel, by God's grace, will be enabled to **look up, and lift up your heads**; knowing our redemption is close at hand.
Luke 21:28

v.12   Total Surrender
The messenger encouraged Daniel by saying that God heard his prayer **the first day.** Daniel wanted to understand what he had seen in the vision, and what would happen to his beloved people, Israel. Now the messenger has come.

Daniel had
- A set heart v.12
- A Purposed Heart v.1:18
- Chastened himself before God v.12

Daniel was totally surrendered to the will of God.

4. The Conflict

v.13   The Rejection
Here the angel messenger pulled back the curtain, so to speak, to show Daniel the struggle in the heavenly realm. Behind the scenes is an unseen war between God and Satan; the angels of God and the demons of Satan; the Spirit of Christ and the spirit of Antichrist. The angel told Daniel that the prince of the Persian kingdom (a fallen angel or evil spirit) had prevented him from getting through with an answer to his prayer.

The evil spirit was so powerful he managed to hold off the good angel for 21 days – the same length of time Daniel had been fasting and praying. Furthermore, the only way the good angel finally got through to Daniel was for Michael, one of the chief angels, to render assistance.

Paul says **we wrestle not against flesh and blood**. *Eph.6:12* The kingdom of Satan is evidently well organized. Here mention is made of **'the prince of the kingdom of Persia'** (in 1935 Persia changed their name to Iran) and in verse 20 of **the prince of Grecia** as well as **the prince of Persia**.

The princes are evidently spirit princes of Satan who act under his jurisdiction and carry out the plans of his organized kingdom. It appears likely that since the world is lying in the lap of the wicked one, and Satan is **'the god of this world'** *2 Cor.4:4*, he has appointed a prince to represent him at each of the national capitals; and that today there is a prince of Iran, a prince of North Korea, and princes of the Nations of the Middle East, a prince of the United States, and of each of the other nations; and these princes, it may well be supposed, have their headquarters at the national capitals where they use their influence to guide legislation and frame policies. It may be also that God has His representatives there too. But the nations, let us not forget, are NOT Christian nations; and so their policies are largely framed under the influence of evil powers. For example: abortion, gay rights movement, same sex marriage. These same princes will lead the nations of the world to Armageddon. *Rev.16:13-16*

The Response

Michael came to help the good angel. Michael is a war angel. He turned up here to help this angel in his struggle with the prince of Persia. He fights for Israel. *Dan.12:1* He disputed with Satan over the body of Moses. *Jude 1:9* He will lead a group of angels that will cast Satan and his angels out of Heaven. *Rev. 12:7*

v.14   The Revelation
The object of the angels communication was to make Daniel know what should befall his people (Israel) *in the latter days*.

v.15   The Reaction
The effect upon Daniel of the angel's word: *I set my face toward the ground* – in reverence rather than in fear. *And I became dumb* – speechless with reverential respect and wonder.

v.16   The confession Daniel made when his mouth was open.

v.17   Both his strength and breath had departed. Daniel could scarcely bear the strain of the contents of the vision; and in this way God would teach His servant his utter weakness; that he might learn that His *strength is made perfect in weakness.* *2 Cor. 12:9*

v.18   The second touch Daniel received and it's effect. The first touch *v. 17* open Daniel's mouth; the second touch strengthened him. He confessed his need and the Lord supplied it.

v.19   The additional strength was afforded as Daniel by faith took what he was told to take.

The Resolution
The angel's remarkable words - which were designed to prepare Daniel for the amazing revelation that was to follow.

v.20 The heavenly messenger departs to carry on the spiritual warfare against the prince of Persia. After he is overcome, the prince of Greece will come; another satanic principality.

v.21 The angel turns Daniel to the Word of God. The Word of God is the only weapon available to the child of God for effective use. It is the Sword of the Spirit.

The following is from The Book of Daniel by W.C. Stevens, "The historical events are not the revelation or the interpretation of the prophecy; they are only its fulfillment, its identification. The historic events derive their light from the prophecy, not the prophecy from the events."

To better understand Chapter 11 of Daniel, we must know historical facts. Some historical books that will help you to understand the historical events are the books of Apocrypha, First Maccabees, and Second Maccabees.

The Apocrypha, not being of Divine inspiration, are not part of the canon of Scripture, therefore, are of no authority in the Church of God. They are only human writings.

First Maccabees is included in the Apocrypha, and is a historical work of great value, giving account of the Jewish wars of independence under the Maccabees family of Levites in the second century B.C.

Second Maccabees is concerned chiefly with Jewish history from the reign of Selevcus IV, 175 B.C., to the death of Nicanor in 161 B.C. It is much less valuable than First Maccabees, though it contacts a good deal of truth. Second Maccabees was written about 125 B.C.

CHAPTER 10

Following are books that I recommend to have as references when studying Chapter 11:

- Illustrated Davis Dictionary of the Bible
- The Four Hundred Silent Years from Malachi to Matthew by H. A. Ironside
- Daniel Verse by Verse Study by Oliver Green

Chapter 11

This chapter gives the most extraordinary and detailed prophecy in the whole Word of God. When we remember that its prophesies; the Reigns of kings, royal marriages, wars, victories, defeats, plots, treaties, assassinations - all show the striking evidence of divine foreknowledge; For who but God could write down such detailed prophecies, which have come true with one exception. The one exception is still future, and awaits fulfillment which will surely come to pass: the coming of the Antichrist.

1. The Continuation

v.1 The same angel as in chapter 10 continues to unfold the prophecies to Daniel. The good angel took a stand to support and protect Darius. It is said he strengthen him. I believe the reason the good angel supported Darius was because Darius was kind to the Jews. He even issued a decree to let them rebuild their Temple in Jerusalem. *Ezra 6:1-18*

v.2 When these words were spoken, Cyrus was King of Persia. After him four other kings were to arise. These four kings were
1. Cambyses – 529-523 B.C.
2. Smerdis – 523-522 B.C. - called 'Fals Smerdis' as he was an imposter who claimed the throne, and reigned only seven months.
3. Darius I Hystaspes – 521-485 B.C. - called 'Darius the Great' as being a great king in Persia history.

CHAPTER 11

4. Ahasuerus – 482-465 B.C. This is the Ahasuerus in the Book of Esther *1:1; 4:1-24* Esther being his second wife.

Ahasuerus was the wealthiest of the four kings. History tells us the following: Darius, King of Persia before Ahasuerus, tried to conquer Greece but was defeated at the Battle of Marathon in 490 B.C. (Marathon was an ancient Greek village in east Attica, or a plain nearby where the Greeks defeated the Persians.) Later when Ahasuerus came to power he sought to avenge this humiliating defeat of Darius. He gathered together a mighty army, estimated at 2,000,000 men, and a navy of many ships to do battle against the Greeks. He crossed the Hellespont (the strait between the Aegean Sea and the Sea of Marmara) and to his great surprise, he too was defeated at the Battle of Salamis (a place in Cyprus) and Thermopylae (in Ancient Greece; a mountain pass on the central east coast). He returned to Persia in shame and humiliation.

2. The Conquer

v.3 The *mighty king* here is Alexander the Great, the king of Greece, who came to power in 335 B.C. He put down Persia *Dan.8:5-6* and assumed world dominion.
Alexander the Great died an alcoholic in 322 B.C. His own posterity did not inherit his vast kingdom.

v.4 Four of his generals divided the empire into four geographical areas over which they ruled.
The division was in the following manner:
- Cassander took Macedonia
- Lysimachus took Asia Minor

- Seleucus Nicator took Syria
- Ptolemy took Egypt

All four families eventually lost their kingdoms when the Romans marched east.

3. The Conflict

The angel focused upon two of the four divisions of Alexander's kingdom, namely, the king of the south (Egypt) and the king of the north (Syria). For the next two to three hundred years these two empires fought each other in a continuous struggle for supremacy. Israel was often caught in the middle and was greatly harmed by their constant fighting; Israel lay between Syria and Egypt.

v.5   The king of the south

South, i.e. south of Palestine, is meant **the king of the south:** Ptolemy I Soter; **and one of his princes** was Seleucus, to whom Syria was given. The latter was stronger that the former and '**his dominion**' was a '**greater dominion**'. Soon the Kings of Egypt and Syrian were fighting each other.

v.6   A Political Marriage

After many years (about 50) the prediction of verse 6 was fulfilled in the marriage of Berenice, daughter of Ptolemy Philadelphus, to Antiochus Theos, third king of Syria, 285-447 B.C. Thus the ruling houses of Egypt and Syria sought to bring about an alliance of political importance; for the father of Berenice gave here in marriage to the king of the north, in order to end his war with the latter.

CHAPTER 11

This Antiochus, in order to marry Berenice, divorced his wife Laodice and disinherited her son. But the marriage of Berenice to Syria's King failed to bring about peace. Ptolemy king of Egypt died; whereupon Antiochus, King of Syria, took back his former wife Laodice. She in turn poisoned him, and put to death Berenice and her son. Laodice then placed her own son, Seleucus Nicator upon the throne.

Wars of Revenge

v.7 A relative of Berenice attacks Syria and prevails. Berenice's brother Ptolemy III, who had become king of Egypt, invades the north (Syria) to avenge his sister's death. His army ravaged the area.

v.8 Ptolemy carried off much plunder and many slaves, as well as the gods of Syria. He took much silver and gold and idols and vessels.

Ptolemy lived about 5 years after the death of Seleucus II of Syria. He had returned home to Egypt because of a palace plot against him. Conflict ceased for some years.

v.9 Egypt was invaded by Seleucus II (242 B.C.) but little came of it and Seleucus returned home (Syria) with nothing to show for the raid.

A Tireless War

v.10 This occurred when the two sons of Seleucus II assemble a great army to move south. The Syrian army would come like a 'flood of soldiers' and reach the strong city of Egypt where the king was. They were seeking to avenge their father's defeat. One of these sons is said to *come, overflow, and pass through*. He is Antiochus III.

v.11 Ptolemy IV Philopater, King of Egypt was aroused to anger. He rose to meet the challenge and defeats Antiochus III. The end was in the 'Battle of Raphia', a town in southwest Palestine, south of Gaza.

v.12 Tremendous battle ensued between Philopater and Antiochus - where the latter was defeated. History shows that Philopater, through love of ease, failed to take up the advantage of his victory. He killed thousands of Syrian soldiers but this would not make Syria give up.

v.13 After some 14 years of progress in the north and decay in the south, Antiochus of Syria makes another invasion of Egypt. He defeats Ptolemy V (who followed Philopater); Philip of Macedonia joins with him. Egypt is defeated 198 B.C.

v.14 Among the many who stood up against Egypt's king at this time were rebels in Egypt and Philip, King of Macedon. *The robbers* of Daniels people were 'apostate Jews' who rebelled against Ptolemy (King of Egypt); joining themselves to Antiochus (King of Syria), hoping thereby to gain independence for Palestine.
to establish the vision; but they shall fall. The Jews helped along the very things which Daniel had predicted, as to trials for them. All this was fulfilled in the severe struggles which followed.

v.15 The king of the south (Egypt) weakens and Antiochus III wins the Battle of Paneas (a city near the source of the Jordan in northern Palestine) and drove the

Egyptians out of Palestine. This significant victory for Syria brought to an end the rule of Egypt in Israel.

v.16 In the course of this conflict the king of the north (Syria; Antiochus) would take the fenced cities in the land of Israel, and *the glorious land* would come under his power. The king of the south (Egypt; Ptolemy) would be unable to stop the conquest of *the glorious land.*

v.17 Antiochus the Great renews his conquest with great success. Antiochus and Ptolemy came to terms and Antiochus gives his daughter Cleopatra to marry Ptolemy, a young man in years. Instead of helping her father, she turns against him and helps her husband Ptolemy. Antiochus hoped that his daughter would undermine the Egyptian government from within and use her position to help him take over. The marriage scheme didn't work.

v.18 Antiochus the Great then turned his face toward the Greek Isles, determined to conquer them. But when he went north to vent his frustration by conquering the Greek Islands, he came into contact with the emerging Roman Empire, which kept him from carrying out his plan.

v.19 Antiochus fled from one fortress to another. He was brought to a halt and put under heavy terms of tribute to Rome.

v.20 This was Antiochus' son, Seleucus IV Philopater who reigned from 187-176 B.C., called a *raiser of taxes* because Rome compelled him to pay yearly taxes. He was soon assassinated by Heliodorus. In his endeavor to raise taxes, he plundered the Holy Temple in Jerusalem.
2.Maccabees.3

4. The Cruel Antiochus Epiphanes

Now we read about one great king of Syria who made and then broke a covenant with Israel. He is a picture of the coming **man of sin.** *2 Thes.2:3-12*

- Near Fulfillment of Prophecy: Antiochus Epiphanes *vs.21-35*
- Future Fulfillment of Prophecy: Man of sin *vs.36-45*

The first part of this prophecy was fulfilled after Daniel died.

The King Antiochus Epiphanes reigned from 175-164 B.C. The messenger told God's Prophet what Antiochus Epiphanes would do to Israel. This is recorded in history books called 1st and 2nd Maccabees, which is not part of the Word of God, but some Bibles include it.

v.21 The Spirit called him *a vile person.* The people did *not give* him the honor of king, but he gained control by lying to the people to make them feel good.

v.22 So Antiochus overthrew those who resisted him, including the high priest, Onias, who was the prince of God's covenant. He put Jason in as high priest. *2.Maccabees 4:4-10.*

v.23 History records that the agreement between this pagan King Antiochus and the high priest Jason was broken, and the king put in a wicked high priest name Menelaus.

v.24 He entered into a rich part of the country and took their money; the earlier kings never did anything like this. Then Antiochus Epiphanes tried to win over others by giving them gifts of money. After this, he planned to enter

CHAPTER 11

and conquer the strong cities, but this was only for a short time.

v.25 War erupted between Egypt (king of the south) and Syria (king of the north).

v.26 Several of Ptolemy's (King of Egypt) key men became corrupted and helped to defeat the king.

v.27 Antiochus Epiphanes sat down with the King of Egypt at a feast to arrange peace, but neither king was sincere.

v.28 Antiochus, after conquering Egypt, returns to Antioch and plundered Palestine and Judea because Jews were supposed to have rejoiced at his supposed death.

v.29 Antiochus invasion and defeat in Egypt are described here and in verse 30. This is the second invasion of Egypt which took place in 168 B.C.; but as predicted it was not successful.

v.30 Met by the Romans near Alexandria, Antiochus was handed a letter from the Roman senate ordering him not to fight with Egypt. When the Syrian King hesitated - the Roman officer drew a circle around Antiochus in the sand and told him he must make a decision before stepping out of the circle. Humiliated, frustrated, and enraged, Antiochus turned back to Syria, having traveled the long distance to Egypt for nothing.

Antiochus persecution of the Jews is described in the following verses. *also see Daniel 8:10-14*

v.31 Again Antiochus stopped in Palestine enroute to Syria, this time venting his frustration and anger against the Jews. Conniving with apostate Jews, he stopped daily sacrifices at the Temple and desecrated the Sanctuary by erecting, in place of the Brazen Altar, a statue of the Greek god Zeus. For the faithful Jews, this was an abomination.

v.32 During these awful days some resisted heroically, led and inspired by the Maccabees. Judas Maccabees eventually led them in a successful revolt. The remnant of Jews who knew God, who believed as did Daniel and his three friends; that God was able to deliver them. These were made strong, and they did '***exploits***' (wage war).

v.33 The revolt of the Jews, though helpful, was never totally successful. Thousands of them were slaughtered.

v.34-35 The suffering of the Jews under Antiochus Epiphanes however had a refining purpose and this refining or purging process is predicted to continue till ***the time of the end***.

This key expression ***the time of the end*** provides the transition from Antiochus Epiphanes to Antichrist; from the past to the future; from history to prophecy. As will be demonstrated, the course of this prophecy changes as the future persecution of Israel in the Tribulation period comes in view. The first 35 verses of this chapter have been fulfilled with amazing accuracy, as would be expected of Divine Revelation. There is every reason to believe, therefore, that the remaining prophecies of this chapter vs.36-45 will have the same precise and literal fulfilled in the future. Israel will continue to be persecuted until the second coming of Christ.
Antiochus Epiphanes died suddenly in 165 B.C.

CHAPTER 11

5. The Coming of the Antichrist

Between verses 35 and 36 there is a gap spanning many centuries; a forward leap from Antiochus Epiphanes to the coming of the Antichrist, the last world dictator *2 Thes.2:3-11; Rev.13:1-10* and the Great Tribulation. *Matt.24:21*

Daniel did not see the New Testament Church-age which has lasted approximately two thousand years. How much longer it will last we do not know.

1. The Character of the Antichrist

v.36
1. He will act in self *will*
The 'willful *king*' is a man completely defiant to the will of God. Satan, as Lucifer, having this character in Isaiah 14:13-14, says five times, *I will ascend…..I will exalt…..I will sit…..I will ascend…..I will be like the most High.* Such an attitude is not unknown in the world today. The *spirit of antichrist* is already in the world; *1 John 4:3* the *mystery of iniquity doth already work.* *2 Thes.2:7*

2. He will *Exalt Himself*
He will *exalt himself* - What a contrast with Jesus Christ who *made himself of no reputation, and took upon him the form of a servant, and was made in the likeness of men.* *Phil.2:7*

3. He will *magnify himself above every god.*
The Antichrist demands to be worshipped and says he is God. *2 Thes.2:4*

4. He will blaspheme the True God
And he opened his mouth in blasphemy against God. *Rev.13:6*

5. He will prosper for a limited period of time.
Even when Antichrist rules, God will control history and permit him to thrive for only a limited period of time (seven years according to Dan.9:24)

v.37
6. He will be an irreligious Person
He will not **regard the God of his fathers**. This is a Jewish expression. I believe the Antichrist will be a Jew since Jesus was a Jew – and the Antichrist will be a counterfeit Christ. **Nor the desire of women**; the Antichrist will very possibly be homosexual.
Nor regard any god: for he shall magnify himself above all. The Antichrist will be his own god.

vs.38-39
7. He will place confidence in military might. The one god the Antichrist will honor is the god of military might – but it is an expensive god, indeed. Antichrist will use his 'god of military might' to dominate the world. Initially, he depended on his charisma, flattery, and talk of peace but now he begins to flex his military muscle.

2. The Conflicts of the Antichrist

v.40 *at the time of the end.*
This reminds us that this is the Great Tribulation period – the 70th week of Daniel.
The king of the south is an evident ruler of Egypt, a leader of the Arab block of nations. This leader will push at the Antichrist, meaning that he will attack him, apparently in an effort to hinder him in his expansionist plans.

CHAPTER 11

The king of the north: a Russian ruler fits well. However since Russia is directly north, with Moscow being almost on a direct north-south line with Jerusalem. Ezekiel 38 describes graphically how God will bring about the destruction of the enemies of His people. A great army with confederates such as ***Persia, Ethiopia, Libya, Gomer***, (Germany) and ***Togarmah*** (Armenia), will assemble, and ***come like a cloud*** on the Holy Land. When the great army falls upon the land, God's fury shall come upon his face. A terrible earthquake will affright man and beast, mountains shall be thrown down, steep places and walls fall down. God will call for a sword.
  Every man's sword shall be against his brother…..pestilence…..overflowing rain, great hailstones fire and brimstone will complete the destruction. *read Ezekiel 38:19-23* This will happen at the end of the first 3 ½ years of the Tribulation. 3 ½ years later will be the Battle of Armageddon at the second coming of Christ. *Rev.19:17-19*

v.41 The Center Stage

God considers Palestine the heart, the center of the whole world. The whole world will suffer under the rule of the Antichrist, but the Middle East will be the major hot spot. The Arabs will want to destroy Israel because of their ancient hatred for them. The Antichrist will want to occupy Israel to protect his oil supplies and to be worshipped in the Temple as God. *2 Thes.2:3-4* Other nations will want to take Israel, so they can drive the Antichrist out and seize the oil for themselves.
The Antichrist will enter the land of Israel and kill many thousands. ***Edom, Moab***, and ***Ammon*** will escape the wrath of the Antichrist. The reference to these three areas are located in the nation we call Jordan. This area will be spared during the Tribulation period. The ancient

city of Petra is located in southern Jordan and it seems to be the place where many Jews will flee during the last half of the Tribulation period, so this may explain why these three areas are spared. **Edom, Moab, and Ammon** have always been enemies of Israel, the Antichrist may spare them, but God will punish them in other ways. At the **time of the end** v.35, 40 all these countries come up again. Ezek.25:4-7; Isa.11:14

v.42 the Doom of Egypt

The Antichrist will defeat and plunder Egypt and Egypt's former allies.

v.43 The Power and Riches

Egypt seems like a poor nation by the world's standards; the ancient treasures of Egypt are among the most valuable in the world. She has many articles of gold and silver on display in many places around the world and, by anyone's standards are priceless.
At his steps i.e. will follow in his steps 'owned as master'.

The Libyans and Ethiopian, nations of Africa will acknowledge that the Antichrist is their Lord and Master.

v.44 the Gathering Storm...
the Road to Armageddon.

The Antichrist will only have a short time to celebrate his victories in Africa. News will reach him that a great army is forming in the east and another is gathering in the north.

The army from the east are:
- China

CHAPTER 11

- Japan
- Mongolia
- India
- All of Eastern Asia *Rev. 16:12*

The Army in the north:
The king of the north is not easily identified. Russia and her allies will have suffered major defeats by this time. The northern army will probably come from many countries around the world, including remnants from Russia, Turkey, Syria, and Lebanon. These all lie north of Israel. At the second coming of Jesus He will stop these nations from destroying the whole earth, and when he does, they will settle their differences, and join their forces together and attack Jesus at Armageddon. *Rev. 19:11-19* **therefore he shall go forth with great fury to destroy, and utterly to make away many.** Although the Antichrist lashes out at the world indiscriminately his anger will be particularly directed towards the Jews.

v.45 the Doom of the Antichrist

The Antichrist hastens back from the land of Egypt, and reaches Palestine where he plants **the tabernacles of his place between the seas** (the Mediterranean Sea and the Dead Sea) **in the glorious holy mountain**; that is Mount Zion (Jerusalem). The Antichrist will be a very proud and powerful, will set himself up to rule the world; will demand and require all men to worship him. *2.Thes.2:4; Rev.13:12* God does not stop him until His time comes; **he shall come to his end, and none shall help him.** Jesus will stop him at Armageddon. The beast and the false prophet - **both were cast alive into a lake of fire burning with brimstone.** *Rev. 19:19-21*

Chapter 12

In this closing chapter we are taken on to the last three and half years that will precede the Thousand year Reign of Christ – The time of the Great Tribulation that will end the sorrows of the Jews and scattering of God's People. *v.7*

1. The Great Tribulation

v.1 Michael the Archangel will help Daniel's people, Israel. God made Michael responsible for His earthly people in a special way. He is the Guardian angel of Israel. *Dan.10:13-21; Rev.12:7-9* Satan hates the nation Israel and had done all in his power to destroy it. There have been many attempts to destroy Israel but it is Michael's responsibility to prevent that.

Behind all the trials they may have to endure, they are assured of the support of spiritual powers in the unseen world. The special call for this spiritual aid will be that, for the Jewish nation, it will **be a time of trouble, such as never was since there was a nation even to that same time**. Nevertheless, this Great Tribulation will end the sorrows of the nation and lead to the deliverance to the godly whose names are found written in the Lambs Book of Life.

2. The Triumph of the Saints

Men must die and return to dust from which God formed Adam. *Gen.2:7-19; Job 34:15* 'Sleep' often means death, *Job 3:13; Ps.13:3* and 'waking up' means rising from death.

CHAPTER 12

Matt.27:52; 1 Corin.15:51; 1 Thes.4:14 All men will rise; some will have eternal life, others eternal death.

v.2   First Resurrection

The first resurrection will be when Jesus comes to rapture the Church. *1 Cor.15; 2 thes.4:13-18* In Revelation 20:5-6 we have the resurrection of the Tribulation Saints, which is called 'part of the first resurrection'. They are raised at the beginning of the 1,000 year reign of Christ. The Church Saints were resurrected approximately 7 years before. The Tribulation martyred are also part of the first resurrection, even though there are approximately 7 years between.

Second Resurrection

When the 1,000 years of Heaven on earth have expired there is the Resurrection of the unsaved who will stand before the Great White Throne to face the Judgment of God. Their sentence is known as the Second Death; The Lake of fire.

v.3   The Wise

The Lord Jesus Christ will catch up His people, the Church and the Saints of the Old Testament, at the Rapture. After that He will give crowns and rewards at the Judgment Seat of Christ *Rom.14:10; 1 Cor.3:13-15; 2 Cor.5:10* to those who have served Him well in this world. *Matt.25:21-23*

3. The Time

v.4 The Sealed Book

These prophecies sealed up (protected) until **the time of the end**. This does not mean the 'end of time', but refers to that definite period of time which in Daniel is the 70th week, or the Great Tribulation. The book was 'sealed' in this sense: the full meaning wouldn't be understood until **the time of the end.** Matt.24:15 **The time of the end** will close with the destruction of the Antichrist when Jesus comes. Rev.19:19-20

Many shall run to and fro. Because the phrase, **to and fro** is a characteristic for world travel, as we behold the communications and transportation networks of our day we do indeed see people running **to and fro.**

And knowledge shall be increased. I believe there is a dual interpretation in this verse.

> **Scientific Knowledge.** Eighty five percent of all scientists who have ever lived are alive today. Three thousand pages of scientific and technological information are being printed every second. Knowledge is doubling every twenty-two months. To try and keep up with this information explosion is impossible. We know the end is coming because people are traveling the world at breakneck speed and knowledge is increasing.
>
> **Prophetic Knowledge.** Historically, none of Daniel's vision made much sense to most Bible scholars until 1890 when Dr. Gabaelein began to teach that the Roman Empire would be revived and play a part in the end times.

CHAPTER 12

Search the writings of Wesley, Luther, Calvin, Moody, and Charles Spurgeon and you will seldom ever see a sermon in print by these men on the second coming of Christ. It is not that Moody, Spurgeon, did not believe in the second coming. They did.   Moody, Spurgeon both were pre-millennial preachers. The reason is that the knowledge of prophecy had not increased in their day as it has in our day. It is a well known fact that during the last 100 years there has been a more intensive study of prophecy than ever before, and coupled with the increased interest in the prophetic Word, there has been a remarkable increase in knowledge concerning the second coming of Jesus Christ.

The Scene at the River

The river is the Hiddekel, Gen.2:14; Dan.10:4 now called the Tigris River.

v.5 Daniel looked and saw two angelic beings; one standing on one bank of the river and the other on the opposite bank. I quote John Phillips in his book on Daniel: "Daniel not only saw the angels. He heard them. These are things that angels desire to look into 1 Pet.1:12 the angelic beings who stand before God, who rush to do His bidding, are intensely interested in Human Affairs."

v.6 *The man clothed in linen* is the pre-incarnate Son of the Living God, Jesus Christ.
Jesus is
- The *Leader* Isa 55:4
- The *Lord of Harvest* Matt.9:38
- The *Lord of Lords* 1 Tim.6:15
- The *Lion of Judah* Rev.5:5
- The *last* Isa.44:6

- The **Lamb of God** John 1:29
- The **Lover** John 13:1
- The **Lily of the Valley** Song.2:1
- The **Lowly in Heart** Matt.11:29
- The **Lord and Saviour** 2 Pet.1:11

The question one of the angels ask was doubtless ask for the benefit of Daniel. *How long shall it be to the end of these wonders?*

v.7   The Solemn Oath

The two hands raised to heaven emphasize the great solemnity of the oath uttered *Gen.14:22; Deut.32:40* **by him that liveth for ever** is an appropriate name for God. *Deut.32:40; 1 Tim.6:16.*

The raising of hands to Heaven was in time of old the most common form of an oath. Thus even the stretching out of the arm obtained the meaning of swearing an oath. *Exod.6:6; Num.14:30* As a rule, however it was done with one hand. *Gen.14:22; Duet.32:40; Rev.10:5*

Why here are both hands raised? Jesus raised both hands as if to say, 'My answer is doubly significant'. It was a way of stressing the surety of His words. In verse 6 one of the angels ask *how long shall it be to the end of these wonders?* The answer to the question: *a time, times, and an half.* This is a reference to the last 3 ½ years of the Great Tribulation. A *time* is one year, *times* 2 years, and *an half*, half a year.

And when he shall have accomplished to scatter the power of the holy people, all these things shall be finished. The word *scatter* here also means to shatter; to dash to pieces; to disperse. The Jews as a nation

CHAPTER 12

rejected Christ at His first coming to earth. *John 1:11* They cried **let him be crucified**. *Matt.27:23*

In 70 A.D. the Romans came and destroyed Jerusalem and the Jews were scattered into the nations of the world. Because of their rebellion against God, He shattered them as a nation. We reap what we sow. *Gal.6:7* For approximately 2000 years Israel was a people without a nation. But it survived. In 1948 again Israel became a nation. They are going back in unbelief; God will use the Great Tribulation to bring them to repentance. I quote John Phillips book on Daniel "They (the Jews) will be reduced to extremity of poverty, weakness, fear, and woe. Never will the world have seen such horrors or such helplessness. They will have no influence, no allies, no hope, no power. They will be brought to an end of themselves. All they have trusted in the past will prove useless. That is what the great tribulation has to accomplish. Then and not until then, will the Lord act. But He knows exactly, to the day, how long it will take: a time, times, and a half."

The Lord will use the Antichrist to humiliate completely the Jewish people. The Lord definitely affirmed that after three and half years of Satan horror, the Israelites will no longer trust in themselves, but in the Lord Jesus Christ, their Messiah. *Rom.11:26; Zech.13:1*

4. The Terminating

v.8   The Puzzled Prophet
Daniel tells us that he **heard, but I understood not**. Daniel wanted an explanation of how the deliverance of Israel will be accomplished. As an Israelite who loved his nation, he was intensely interested in that.

v.9 The Proper Time

The time of the end. Daniel is bidden to go his way, as *the words are closed up and sealed till the time of the end.* God tenderly and lovingly reminded Daniel that his purpose would ripen fast. There was nothing for him to worry about. He need not have any fear of the future. He had no need to be uneasy as God was in total control of the situation. God told Daniel this was all he needed to know at the present time. There was no need for him to know all the details for the revelation would not be fulfilled in his lifetime.

> The Time was Set
> The Truth was Sealed
> The Triumph was Sure

v.10 The Purified

During this terrible time there will be those who will not bow to the Antichrist, but through these testings they will come out pure and white and without a fault. However the wicked shall increase in their wickedness, and they shall not understand; i.e. act without understanding. The growing divide between the wicked and the wise becomes sharper and wider. But wise people will understand that the end is near.

Three Periods of time

These three periods of time are still in the future. 1260 – 1290 – 1335.

v.11 *the abomination that maketh desolate* is when the Antichrist sits in the Temple of God and demands to be worshipped as God. *Matt.24:15; 2.Thes.2:3-4.* ***There shall be a thousand two hundred and ninety days.***

CHAPTER 12

The Jews counted a month 30 days, so a year was 360 days. In this way three and a half years would be 1260 days; *Rev.11:3* so there will be another 30 day added after the Lord comes until He sets everything in order. The added 30 days goes beyond the end of the Tribulation. The Great Tribulation will last for 1260 days or 3 ½ years; then Jesus will come. *Rev.19:11-21* The 1260 days are the closing half of the Great Tribulation.

v.12 Those who wait and come to the period are characterized as **blessed**. *Matt.25:34* This **blessed** state is no doubt the commencement of the Millennial Reign of our blessed Lord on the earth.

With regard to the 1335 days in this verse; this is 1260 days with an addition of 75 days. This again being an addition of 45 days beyond the 1290 of verse 11. 1335 is therefore 1260 + 30 + 45. Prior to Christ setting up His Millennial kingdom on earth is a 75 day interval probably for the Judgment of the Nations and Israel *Mat.25:31-34; Ezk.20:35-38* and the clean up of the earth after Armageddon.

v.13   The Personal Prophecy

Daniel life was drawing to a close. The prophecy ends with a kindly personal prophecy to the aged prophet. The exhortation to the believer in Christ is exactly the same.

In youth, strike the path that God desires as Daniel did.

- ***Go thy way***; that is the Way, the Work, the Walk, the Will appointed by God. Daniel Did. If in the peak of life, steadfastly maintain a faithful course. If in old age persevere to the finish line, complete course. *2 Tim.4:6-8*

- *Till the end be*; though a great man of God, Daniel was to enter into death like all men.

- *For thou shalt rest;* in death – not soul sleep. Daniel would rest in the comfort of God and rest from his labors. *Rev. 14:13*

- *Stand;* i.e. raised from the dead

- *In thy lot at the end of the days;* though his body would lie in death at the end of his days, yet he would stand in resurrection *at the end of the days* and receive his allotted inheritance.

Amen.

BIOGRAPHY

Daniel – by A. C. Gaebelin

Prophecies of Daniel – by Lehman Strauss

Daniel – Verse by Verse – by Oliver B. Green – (Excellent on Chapter 11)

Daniel – Verse by Verse – by Harold B. Sightler

A Devotional Study of the Book of Daniel – by J. Allen Blair

The Prophet Daniel – by R. E. Harlow

Commentary on Daniel – by Harry Bultema

Exploring the Book of Daniel – by N. W. Hutchings

Daniel and His Prophecy – by Frederick A. Tatford

Daniel & Revelation Made Plain – by Mark Cambron

Delving Through Daniel – by J. Vernon McGee

The Book of Daniel – by John Heading

The Prophecies of Daniel – by Louis T. Talbot

Daniel – by H. A. Ironside

The Book of Daniel – by W. C. Stevens

The Book of Daniel – by Rev. Clarence Larkin

Studies in Daniel – by J. Narver Cortner

www.ingramcontent.com/pod-product-compliance
Lightning Source LLC
Chambersburg PA
CBHW070453100426
42743CB00010B/1608